The
STEM Student
Survival Guide

(162)

Don't let your kid go to college until you _both_ read this book!

Leon Roomberg, MS, PMP, MDBA
"The Most Dangerous Man in Higher Education"

This book may be purchased in bulk for educational, business, or sales promotional use. For information, please fill out the form at: email **www.thestemstudentsurvivalguide.com/feedback**.

Published by Leon Roomberg, 304 Garwood Place, Cherry Hill, New Jersey 08003 USA

Library of Congress Cataloging-in-Publication Data
Names: Roomberg, Leon 2017 – Author
Title: The STEM Student Survival Guide
Description: First United States Edition. | Cherry Hill, New Jersey: Leon Roomberg, 2017

ISBN 978-0-9991900-0-5 (Paperback Edition)
ISBN 978-0-9991900-1-2 (Ebook Edition)
ISBN 978-0-9991900-2-9 (Hardcover Edition)

First United States Edition
10 9 8 7 6 5 4 3 2 1

Identifiers: [1. STEM Education. 2. STEM. 3. Self-Help]

Library of Congress Control Number: 2017910973

Dedications

For Susan. Thirty-eight years of love, joy, and my ally against life's challenges.

For Catie, Skye, Zachary, Jerry, Justin, and Ryan. For bringing new perspectives and contentment into my life.

For the "Castaways" and my other friends and relatives who share my love of geeky conversation.

For Grandmom Sadie and her one relentlessly mind-warping "joke."

For the family and other friends who edited, respectfully criticized, and helped me make this a better book. (Especially Lisa and Ginny.)

And especially to the <u>high school and college counselors, advisors, teachers, and administrators</u> with the courage and honesty required to insist their students and parents read this book.

Leon J Roomberg

✓ First, understand there are people whose jobs,
  and institutions whose existence, depend on
  manipulating your actions.

✓ Second, understand that most of the people
  who will teach in your classroom are underpaid
  and not incented to focus on your success.

✓ Third, understand that there are actions you can
  take to ensure your own success despite your
  immersion in a corrupt and incompetent
  education system.

About the Author

Growing up prior to the popularization of the term "ADHD," teachers classified Leon Roomberg as "trouble."

Due to financial challenges, he attended six different colleges intermittently. He earned Bachelor and Master degrees from the University of Bridgeport, certifications in Project Management and Database Administration, then attended doctoral courses at three different colleges.

Leon is fortunate to have had many mentors including his father, Gerald "Jerry" Armon Roomberg, David Hess, Brad Calcagni, Lou Krassen, Bill Korn, and Beryl Wolk.

Leon has four decades of technical, managerial, and executive experience, serving companies large and small, hiring more than a hundred people in both intern and professional roles, mentoring more than a dozen. He founded several small businesses and maintained a non-profit counseling practice.

Leon lives in New Jersey, with his wife and love of his life, Susan. They have four grown children, two son-in-laws, three grandchildren, and two Bedlington Terriers. (Bedlingtons are the best breed of the known universe.)

It was during more than two dozen father-son college tours that the ideas for his book, "The Stem Student Survival Guide," took form.

Teachers still think he is "trouble."

Errata (Errors and Corrections)

Recognized Errors, Corrections, Missed Acknowledgments, and Apologies made after publication of this edition can be found at www.thestemstudentsurvivalguide.com/errata.

If you find something I need to correct or otherwise atone for, please send your suggestions by using the web page,

www.thestemstudentsurvivalguide.com/feedback.

Image Licensing

Some of the images in this book are licensed from www.iStockPhotos.com. (They are each footnoted as [162].) A comprehensive list including iStockPhoto IDs, and descriptions, can be found in the "References" section at the end of the book.

CONTENTS

Attention Parents & Students:

Not Everything is Bad

In the following pages, you will read a "whole lot of bad stuff" about mistreatment of students by colleges.

My research shows that this mistreatment occurs in the majority of the more than 3,000 U.S. colleges, including elite schools, state schools, private schools, and even community colleges.

However, that same research uncovered more than 150 colleges where small groups of teachers are taking action to reduce some of these abuses. There are even some "pockets of excellence" hidden within some colleges whose overall behavior toward STEM students is abusive.

I am sure there are other colleges that are taking such actions quietly, out of sight of the press. By the time you read this, perhaps your college (or prospective college, or former college) will have done so as well. Maybe even some of the colleges I call out by name in the book.

Before you trust your time and money and future debt to any college, you need to ask a few relevant questions.

This is not a book about condemning an entire industry because of "a few bad apples." It is about actions you can take to succeed in getting your degree despite an imperfect system.

CHAPTERS
FOR
STUDENTS & PARENTS

Introduction

(162)

Are you thinking of a career in STEM (**S**cience, **T**echnology, **E**ngineering, **M**ath, or **M**edicine)? My friend, if you are a student, the education system is stacked against you. This book shows students and their parents what they are up against and how to succeed despite a corrupted university system. Colleges take your tuition, provide inadequate education, and then blame the students when forty to sixty percent of them fail out in the first two years, resulting in student financial losses and sometimes-permanent damage to individual self-esteem.

In the immediate term, this book provides strategies on how to **select less incompetent schools** and then how to succeed in them despite the level of incompetent education you will experience. From **course selection to course scheduling**; from **selecting your peers and study groups** to **selecting your tutors**, this book gives you strategies to be part of the fifteen to twenty percent who graduate in six years or less and graduate without forfeiting your college aid. For these reasons alone, high school juniors, seniors, college students, and their parents, need to read this book before making decisions about college they will regret for the rest of their lives.

In the medium and longer term, this book includes a roadmap of how to fix what is broken for those college administrators, lawmakers, and regulators, who possess the courage to do so.

As a business person who learned to "Manage by Exception," I wrote this book by focusing on solving problems. Do not let those challenges discourage you from a STEM education. The rewards to you and to society far outweigh four to six years of personal and financial stress.

This book addresses big issues and promotes a number of tactics that students (and their supportive families) can use to increase the odds of academic success. Not every tactic applies to everyone. If I make an observation or suggest a tactic that conflicts with your world-view, just leave it aside and embrace those that make sense for your situation. I get enough hate mail as it is and understand that change upsets people. If you can disagree without being disagreeable, I welcome your comments and suggestions for improvements in future editions of the book at **www.thestemstudentsurvivalguide.com/feedback**.

About the phrase "fail out."

Wherever in the text you see the phrase "fail out," it refers to students that have not just failed a course, but have been voluntarily or involuntarily removed from the STEM program they chose to study. Some students will then pursue an "easier" path in the Liberal Arts or Business. Some will drop out of college, often taking with them lower self-esteem and a lifetime of college debt.

One of my editors hates this phrase. However, it is the shortest yet clearest way I have found to describe this preventable and obnoxious result of our corrupt educational system.

About the terms "school," "college," and "university."

In this book, these terms are used interchangeably. They refer to institutions that grant bachelor's degrees.

If I am referring to "High School" or "Graduate School," I will not use informal abbreviations.

Motorcycle Kits

(162)

Imagine there is a club of people, who drive and enjoy highly specialized off-road motorcycles originally sold as kits. The club members appear to be smart, but not necessarily smarter than you, or your parents, or most of your friends. You decide to join the club.

You visited various dealerships who each claimed they offered the best experience for buying the kits for this highly specialized off-road vehicle. Some dealers have gourmet coffee lounges. Some have kitchenettes in their lounges. Some have gyms in the back where you can pass the time waiting for your motorcycle kit delivery. Some sponsor sporting events to entertain you during your free time.

You finally select the dealer who made you feel most at home and said you were ready to buy the motorcycle kit. The salesperson agrees to sell you this motorcycle kit under two conditions. First, you must take a basic mechanic's course. Then, you must score highly on an exam. These steps assure the dealer that you are competent and have the skills to assemble the kit.

You took the prerequisite course and the exam and your grades in both were high enough that the salesperson consented to sell you that vehicle for between $50,000 and $200,000, depending on the features of a given model.

From the beginning, you struggled to assemble the vehicle. While the salesperson said they would grant you some office visits and maybe even some extra tutoring, their bottom line message was that if you could not assemble the motorcycle, then you must be too dumb, or too lazy, or maybe the required prerequisite course you took really didn't teach you what you needed to know.

After two years of hard work, you gave up. The salesperson said you are not entitled to any kind of refund or credit toward another purchase because they do not give refunds to people who are too stupid, or too lazy, or too ill prepared to assemble their motorcycles.

You did a little research on the web and found that depending on the dealer, between forty and sixty percent of their customers were never able to assemble their motorcycles. No dealer ever admitted to selling a defective product.

In addition, of the motorcycle buyers who succeeded in assembling their motorcycles, the majority took five or six years to do so, despite the dealers' beautiful web sites and brochures explaining how to complete the assembly in only four years.

(Also, the costs buyers actually paid went up by as much as fifty percent by taking five or six years to complete assembly.)

After all, depending on the dealer, between forty and sixty percent of their customers succeeded in assembling their motorcycles. So of course, the problem must be with customers who are too stupid, or too lazy, or too ill prepared.

What does this have to do with a STEM education? Oh boy.

(162)

Helicopter Parenting vs. Partnership Parenting

In recent years, there has been a lot of press about "Helicopter Parents."

---

helicopter parent

1. The bane of the dean's existence. The parent who hovers and flaps his wings while the kid lives in his shadow. Particularly prevalent at high-priced colleges, where parents feel obliged (or entitled) to intervene on issues down to the candlepower of the lightbulbs.

Yes, helicopter parent, your intentions are good, but that rotor of yours is causing a din.--Felix Carroll, Albany Times Union, January 27, 2005

2. Parents that hover over their children, hawkishly "helping" them face the college learning scenario. It is debated whether or not parents that hover are good or bad for their child's overall development.

From the Urban Dictionary [135]

Some frustrated educators have expressed that that the Helicopter Parents' "hovering" is in itself what is delaying their offspring from maturing from adolescents to young adults.

There are two reasons this concern is misplaced. (And why the information here is the concerned parent's tool (weapon?) to insure their child successfully graduates from college.)

First, there is our evolving understanding of the brain development process.

… the BBC reports that British psychologists have established new medical guidelines for the end of adolescence, moving the age of entry into adulthood from 18 to 25 years of age.

In part, the new British guidelines were informed by neurobiology, specifically the relatively recent discovery that the prefrontal cortex of the brain does not fully mature until age 25. The prefrontal cortex governs executive functioning; decision making, problem solving, understanding future consequences, and impulsivity. If this area of the brain is not grown up until 25, it makes sense that the years of the early twenties are [now understood to be] the final stage of adolescence. [136]

Second, as discussed in later chapters, about half of all STEM students will fail out within twenty-four months. They will fail out not because they did poorly in high school; in fact, they did well. They will fail out not because they had poor SAT scores; in fact, they were well above average. They will fail out not because they are lazy or stupid; in fact, they spent more than double the time of their liberal art majoring peers on homework.

They will fail out because the majority of colleges in the U.S. abuse their students with incompetent practices and then blame the students when they fail. Through a partnership that includes both parent and student, actions can be taken to increase the odds of success.

It is for these reasons that parents need to read this book first and then **partner** with their kids to plan on succeeding despite a system that is set up to fail about half of their students.

One of my editors was concerned about the "voice" of the text. When should it speak to parents? When should it speak to students? Both parents and students need to read every section. Then they can partner in the great and unexpectedly expensive adventure that is college.

Why College for a STEM Career?

Assuming your personality and intellect are a match for whatever career you are studying for, here are my list of the most important reasons to pursue a STEM career:

1. It's What Society Needs

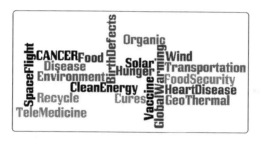

We need scientists to invent cures for diseases, invent less expensive energy that does not harm the environment, create clean drinking water, grow healthy food, and figure out how we are to deal with Global Warming. We need Engineers and Technologists to turn those discoveries into practical solutions. We need Health Care Providers to take care of an aging population.

In short, while we also need Liberal Arts and Business majors, we desperately need more STEM professionals. That is why we compensate them so well for putting up with such an expensive, stressful, and incompetent educational system.

Despite all of these positive reasons, the number of people successfully completing STEM college programs is barely increasing. As reported in the New York Times (and originally in Investors' Business Daily):

Over the past 25 years, the total number of students in college has increased by about 50 percent. Nevertheless, the number of students graduating with degrees in science, technology, engineering, and math (the so-called STEM fields) has been flat…

If students are not studying science, technology, engineering, and math, what are they studying? In 2009, the United States graduated 89,140 students in the visual and performing arts, more than in computer science, math and chemical engineering combined and more than double the number of visual and performing arts graduates in 1985. [34]

2. Money

With few exceptions, most STEM careers pay more money than most careers resulting from a Liberal Arts or Business education.

While money isn't everything in life, it does help with food, clothing, shelter, insurance, internet, educating one's children, and the ability to write a check when a family member is in need or a public disaster causes the Red Cross to beg for donations. Money may not buy happiness, but it sure can prevent or resolve a lot of misery.

Adopted from Anthony P. Carnevale, Nichole Smith, Michelle Melton, STEM *Endnote* [104]

3. Job Satisfaction & Happiness

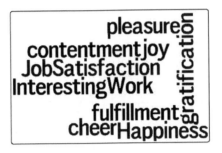

If your passion is to teach art or English, please do so. However, there are thousands of careers that fall under the STEM umbrella that make people happy while spending their workday solving problems that help the economy, and/or society, and/or the environment.

Murray Nichol of The World Economic Forum published a study titled, *"Are These the World's Best Jobs?"* [109] In the study, people in various professions were surveyed as to how happy they are with their job and with their work/life balance. Look at the following diagram and you will see that the majority of jobs with happy workers are in fact, STEM professions:

What People Who Enjoy Their Jobs Earn

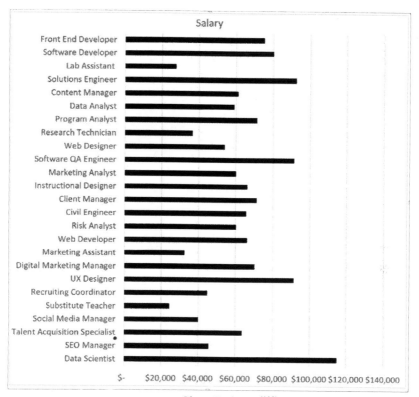

Chart Endnote [109]

The chart shows that while money is not everything (lowly paid Substitute Teachers and Marketing Assistants are included), that the vast majority of people on this list of happy people have STEM careers.

4. Job Security

The Great Recession officially lasted from 2007 through 2009. For many, the changes in the economy meant multiple years of unemployment. However, this was not generally the case for most people in STEM professions. In most locales, the STEM unemployment rarely exceeded two per cent and even then, STEM professionals willing to relocate usually found well-paying replacement jobs fairly quickly.

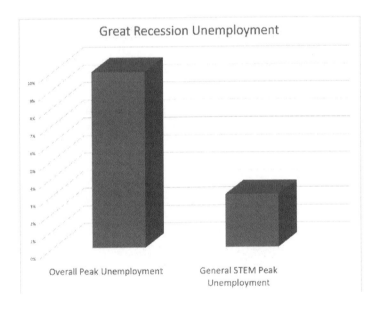

5. Career Launch

(162)

The well-spoken young woman who waits on me at my favorite bagel shop has a Liberal Arts degree in Marketing with a specialization (but not a major) in statistical analysis. She earns little more than minimum wage and has few benefits.

With absolutely no experience, the starting salary for STEM graduates in the most popular fields START between $55,000 and $70,000 per year and most increase every year thereafter. A STEM education often costs roughly the same as a Liberal Arts education. Consider this: 36% of 18- to 31-year-olds were living at home in 2012. How many of these were STEM graduates struggling to pay their student loans? I bet not many. If the young woman in question had reversed her concentrations and majored in Math and minored in Marketing, her income would probably be doubled (or better) than what she currently earns.

Consider, for a moment, the state of Massachusetts. The state's two and one half million households have the second highest per-capita income in the United States, [125] trailing only

Connecticut. Of the state's six and one half million residents, (126) five and one-half million are of working age. (127) The state has low unemployment. (128) Why? The state has the highest percentage of residents with a college degree as compared to the other 49 states. Thanks to the reputation of the Massachusetts Institute of Technology (among others), the state is a magnet for companies employing STEM professionals. As a result, residents of that state suffered less during the recession than almost anywhere else.

We know about high wages paid to STEM graduates. What about everyone else? More than 800,000 workers in Massachusetts earn less than $11 per hour. (Of these, about 330,000 workers earn less than $9 per hour.) (90)

The real shock comes when we examine the composition of the low-wage work force. One in four have some type of college degree while 28% have at least some college.

About Half of Low-Wage Workers Have Attended College

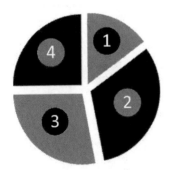

1. Less than High School 15%
2. High School Degree 32%
3. Some College   28%
4. AA,BA, or Higher 25%

Source: Adapted from Economic Policy Institute analysis of Current Population Survey, Outgoing Rotation Group, 2011-2012. Chart Endnote (90)

I wonder how many of those low-wage college graduates will ever pay off their student loans, leave their parents' homes, marry, and buy their own home.

There is a lot that is wrong with STEM education that this book exposes. Do not get too discouraged. The reasons above should be reason enough to take the suggestions here on how to succeed.

There are always exceptions

I have a son-in-law who has a liberal arts degree who is working to create clean drinking water, grow healthy food, and figure out how we are to deal with Global Warming. The existence of people like him and Steve Jobs and others who did not obtain STEM degrees only mean that for exceptional people, there is always a way to pursue goals that address these problems.

However, if you do not have the combined intellect and luck of a Steve Jobs, then pursuit of a STEM profession gives you great odds of both personal financial rewards and service to humanity.

Attention non-STEM students and parents

This book is not about "putting you down". Many of my undergrad studies were general liberal arts and business courses. The same goes for much of my graduate course work.

Both of my daughters and both of their husbands studied Liberal Arts. Each of them are making contributions that are more substantial to our society than I ever will.

This reason this book focuses on the STEM community is the inexcusable failure rates among STEM students. (But if you get some benefit out of the recommendations, or want to respectfully suggest an improvement or correction for a future edition, drop me an email and let me know at www.thestemstudentsurvivalguide.com/feedback)

Assumptions

From the student's perspective, this book gives you the tools to succeed within the STEM educational system as it is today.

The book does not challenge in any way that the curriculum or standards for STEM majors as defined by nationally recognized and accepted organizations. If the authorities say that your major requires Calculus III or Organic Chemistry, then so be it.

The book assumes that for most STEM courses, there either currently exists or can easily be developed, exams that are independent of any one institution that can be accepted by regionally and professionally accredited organizations as proof of mastery for most courses.

The book assumes that the existing graduation requirements for any given STEM major should not change.

The book assumes that teachers successfully improve the quality of education they provide when given reasonable metrics, feedback, workload, and compensation.

Lastly, the book assumes our educational system goal should be to graduate as many fully qualified STEM students as possible.

More than Two Dozen College Tours

(162)

Neither of my daughters needed any help from me in selecting a college. Skye, discovered Prescott College in Arizona. Prescott turned out to be the perfect vehicle for someone committed to serving humanity and the environment through an incredible Liberal Arts education. She later selected the University of New Mexico for her Masters and SUNY (the State University of New York,) for her Ph.D. studies. Catie, also went to Prescott and the school was a perfect fit for her commitment to serving humanity and the environment as well.

Zachary is my oldest son. He is a computer and math whiz. He was open to researching and touring colleges as a father-son adventure. Jerry is a chemistry, math, and business whiz. Four years younger than Zach, he too was open to jointly touring and discussing the merits of various colleges.

I thought I was in a good position to be of help in this adventure. Over the last 35 years, I have hired and/or managed more than 200 people. Most of those jobs were for technology positions that required college backgrounds. I learned which colleges, especially those in the North-East states, generally sent me graduates prepared for the challenges of the workplace.

In addition, my own nineteen-year journey of part-time college enabled me to experience one or more courses at eight different colleges. That meant experiencing the recruitment process at each of those colleges as well.

I changed my major more than once and including graduate school, took more than sixty courses. (I subsequently took more than 20 courses at technical trade schools in programming, database administration, network administration, and operating system administration.)

If anyone could help sniff out good colleges for technology positions, who was in a better position than me?

We visited more than a dozen state colleges in five different states on both sides of the country. We also visited more than a dozen private colleges in those states.

So here, in one chapter, you get to experience the essence of more than two dozen college tours.

Most colleges have online reservations for tours. Your tour-guide will often be an outgoing and enthusiastic junior or senior who has been trained on where to take you and what to discuss. With good timing, you will be able to sign up to tour with families of similar majors.

Most of what you see on your tour will have nothing to do with the quality of education. Instead, your tour usually focuses on the quality of campus life. On our tours, I discovered:

- The outdoor swimming pools and indoor exercise rooms at the University of Arizona would be acceptable to most millionaires.

- School spirit at Penn State and Rutgers is incredible.

- The variety of athletic offerings at Lafayette includes Frisbee Golf.

- Some schools have house cleaners who will not only clean your dorm, but will take your dirty laundry as well.

- The cafeteria at Rowan (at least during the week) serves a wonderful variety of both healthy and comfort food. (In time, Jerry came to disagree with this statement.)

- The engineering and chemistry labs at many of these schools display millions and millions of dollars of impressive-looking equipment.

- The number of schools with recently built engineering or chemistry buildings that cost more than sixty million dollars to create is truly impressive.

(Side rant because I can't wait for later)

If the education provided by these schools were equivalent, then perhaps any of the above items would be legitimate reasons to choose one college over another. However, the quality of STEM education at even the most well-known of these schools varies wildly.

What difference does it make that one school has better food or school spirit if they have STEM failures of between forty and sixty percent?

"Oh no," you may think. "Not my son or daughter. My offspring is intelligent, hardworking, well adjusted, and motivated. They graduated in the top quarter of their high school class and scored in the top quarter of SAT exams in the country. I bet the STEM failure students are in the bottom half of their high school classes."

Mom and Dad, I have bad news for you. The STEM students in general are from the top half if not the top third of their high school classes. They generally did well on their SAT exams. The problem is NOT with the kids. It is with a defective educational offering that abuses about half of the kids in these programs.

(162)

At some point on every tour, you will sit through a presentation and slide show about your particular program. I have now experienced more than two dozen such presentations.

In every presentation, the professors and administrators do their best to welcome you and make you feel welcome at their school. After all, each student represents between $50,000 and $200,000 of revenue. (Once you add in room, board, books, entertainment, and miscellaneous charges, this is the true range of college prices for a four-to-six-year bachelor's degree.)

You will see slides and videos of kids in the classroom, kids on the ball field, and kids in the library. You may hear from energetic students who testify how wonderful their college career has been to-date. You are hearing from motorcycle kit salespeople who are often omitting the real experiences of the majority of students in their STEM programs who are in the process of failing out or have already failed out.

Before I unfairly condemn an entire profession, there were a few presentations where the professors or deans tried in a tactful, albeit subtle manner, to be honest about what they were selling. There were several colleges whose deans knew that their educational offerings were better than their competitors' offerings. Those deans made clear and convincing arguments as to why.

I took copious notes at each of these presentations. What follows is a paraphrased consolidation of the best speeches from the deans of the best colleges. I have added some warnings based on research that is more recent. No college has every advantage listed here. Not every dean admitted every listed deficiency. But you are about to learn in a few minutes of reading what took me more than forty-eight days of on-site college visits to learn.

While the speeches were targeted toward engineers, chemistry, and computer science majors, they apply equally well to almost every STEM profession.

The Deans' Consolidated Speech

(The following speech is a fictional consolidation of the speeches my sons and I heard during our college tours. The speech that follows is written as if presented by a truthful, open, and honest dean of one of the better colleges.)

Parents and prospective students, welcome to our university and associated colleges. You have already heard from some of our professors and current students. Now it is my turn.

I would like to be able to tell you that our curriculum is better than our competitors' curriculum. I would like to be able to tell you our teachers are better than our competitors' teachers. I would like to be able to tell you that we have a better library and better research facilities than at any of our competitors.

However, if I told you any of these things, I would not be telling you the truth.

Standardized Curriculum

(162)

Here, then, is the truth. Our college is regionally accredited. More importantly from your perspective, professional authorities accredit our various STEM programs. National bodies set the curriculum for most of our engineering, science, technology, and medical majors many years ago. As a result, there is little difference between colleges in the courses offered.

For example, to earn a bachelor's degree in Electrical Engineering, the student will take ten courses each year for a total of forty courses over four years. In each year, there may at most, one or maybe two "elective" courses as opposed to the eight or nine other courses they will take. The list of all of those courses is on our web site. Our list of courses will generally match the offerings of all the other regionally accredited universities for your major.

If a student majors in Electrical Engineering and minors in Math as we recommend, the three Math courses will replace the electives and the course load will be almost identical no matter where your student attends.

Similar Quality of Instruction

(162)

With regard to the teaching staff, every school will tell you that they think their teachers are the best. In fact, the standards for those teachers are very high and set by the same national accreditation body. All colleges are competing in the same job market to hire the most qualified teachers.

There is no shortage of qualified teachers. According to the Economist magazine, ninety percent of teachers with doctorates who desire a full-time tenured teaching position never get that position because of the enormous over-supply of qualified professionals. [50]

Do not focus too much on how most schools brag about their professors. Part-timers, graduate students, and full timers who wish they were tenured professors, teach most of the classes across the nation.

The national accrediting organizations set the rules for everyone's libraries and research facilities so there is often no real difference to your educational outcomes there either.

The Marketing Pitch

So, some schools will sell you on applying to them not because they have the best education, but because they represent they offer a "typical" education coupled with great recreation, delicious food, great school spirit, and other amenities to pamper their students.

That may be good enough for them, but in our college, there are differences in the education that I am going to reveal to you today.

What You Are Actually Paying For

[*The fictional dean's speech continues.*]

Depending on the college you attend, each of those forty courses will cost about the same amount of money no matter the class size. (Yes, four credit courses technically cost more than three credit courses, but for our discussion, we divide the four-year cost by the forty courses.) When you factor in room and board, books, and the revocation of aid and scholarships that I will tell you about later, most state colleges cost about $2,000 per course and at our private college, the cost is about $4,400 per course.

Depending on the university in question, the percentage of STEM students who fail out or drop out in the first two years typically ranges between forty and sixty percent.

Almost all regionally accredited colleges are selective on who we admit to our programs so our freshman classes are generally composed of well-educated and well-prepared students.

When I say fail out or drop out, that does not mean that all those who do are so discouraged that they never graduate from college. Many will start again in an easier program such as business or Liberal Arts and finish in six or seven years.

However, to fail out during the first two years can be an expensive learning experience. Depending on how many semesters it took to drop out, the financial loss can be between $25,000 and $125,000.

Unfortunately, some of those who drop out will be so discouraged that they will never complete college in any form. Statistically speaking, those dropouts will generally earn low wages and struggle with their student loans for decades to come.

I am going to illustrate several items that set this college apart from many others. These items are the reasons our success rate of freshman who graduate with degrees in engineering is often close to the sixty percent level of better colleges. If you are doing your job as a responsible consumer, you will ask about these three items on every college tour you take.

Hands-on Involvement
[*The dean's speech continues.*]

(162)

The first differentiator that makes our college, so wonderful is more hands-on involvement. The classes, including the required labs, are set in the standard curriculums for each major. Typically, most STEM students at other universities will have between two and three hours per week of lab time. At our college, when not in class or participating in some sports activity, you will spend much of the rest of your time in some campus lab putting your classroom exercises into physical (hands-on) work.

Your first week of class as a freshman here, you will be given a welder's mask and safety instruction. *Our* freshmen spend a self-reported *AVERAGE* of ten to fifteen *hours per week* welding model steel bridges, or building robots, or concrete canoes, or any number of other hands-on activities in our labs.

STEM courses are tough. However, lots of hands-on work by students in labs is important. That activity helps convey difficult concepts. At the same time, that activity keeps up morale by simulating the fun part of real-world work. Daily extensive lab time is one of the reasons our school is so effective.

When touring those state colleges with the regionally and professionally accredited programs, you may find the multi-million-dollar engineering labs are awe-inspiring. Ask your guide how much time undergrads spend with hands-on work in those labs. In many, the truthful answer is that those pretty labs are for graduate students and their professors only. The actual labs open for undergrads to use are often be insignificant and toy-like in comparison, and access limited to a few hours per week during official lab time. Just think, some of those great schools with great reputations and school spirit report lab time of only two to three hours per week. The colleges who compete with us should all be ashamed of themselves. [*The dean's speech continues.*]

No Lecture Halls for STEM Students

The second differentiator has to do with class size. STEM classes are challenging and compared to other majors, have high failure rates. Our students deserve the help and attention of their teacher.

(162)

Really, how much learning is really accomplished in a lecture hall?

We Have Plenty of Income

(We just have interesting spending priorities.)
[The dean's speech continues.]

With 40 students, a state college earns about $80,000 of total revenue (includes tuition, room, board, state and federal funding, corporate donations, and endowment contribution) per course and a private school such as ours earns about a $160,000 of revenue per course. Even if half of that money has to pay for dorms, food, and recreation, there appears to be plenty of money to pay for the teacher, the use of the school building, and the cost of school administrators. With all this revenue, there should be funds for graduate students to tutor those who need help.

Most full-time teachers teach three courses in the fall and three courses in the spring. That means the annual revenue attributable to each teacher at a public university is about $480,000 and almost a million dollars a year at private schools such as ours.

The Competitors vs. Us
[*The dean's speech continues.*]

Let us look at how many of our competitors are teaching. Some of the most famous state schools in our area will provide up to half of the 20 courses in the first two years in a lecture hall format. Lecture halls often have 300 to 500 students.

Even in a school with only 200 students in a lecture hall, what kind of help is available to individual students? Help from Graduate Students! That is what your money pays for at other colleges.

The majority of classes taught at many colleges are taught by part time teachers and graduate students who may or may not be competent teachers. As most are paid poverty level wages, how much time outside of class do you think they make available to their struggling students? [Editor- The claims in this paragraph are documented later in this book.]

At 200 students, state schools get almost a half million dollars in tuition for each lecture hall class and private schools like ours get over a million tuition dollars per lecture hall class. This means the students who pay for lecture hall classes pay just as much money, but receive a tiny fraction of attention they would receive in a regular classroom.

What kind of failure rate do you expect from a class with forty students as compared to class with two hundred to six hundred students?

I wish I could tell you that our university has no lecture hall classes. In fact, the Liberal Arts and Business students have many. However, this is not the case for our STEM students. Even in a crowded course, there will never be more than forty-four students in a classroom and for most courses, even less than that.

Class size caps and no lecture hall classes for STEM students, are other reasons our students fail less frequently than at other colleges. [Dear reader, the claims in the above paragraph were made by only two out of all the colleges we toured.]

(162)

Above: Lecture Hall vs. Class Room – Same Price!

Two colleges; each are teaching the same course; and each charge the exact same tuition. One presents the course in a lecture hall with hundreds of students. One teaches the course in a classroom with twenty-two students. Can you guess which college fails 60% of the class and which college typically fails less than 10%?

College English in College Classrooms
[The dean's speech continues.]

(162)

The third differentiator is that our teachers are fully and completely competent in conversational English. This may seem like an obvious requirement for courses taught in the United States, but a quick scan of student complaints on websites like "RateMyProfessor.com" shows that for many students, the teacher's English language skill deficiencies meant the tuition paid for a course was a complete waste of money. Unlike some other colleges, we value fame in the world of research in no way as compensating for deficiencies in teaching skills. We believe that English fluency is the most important of those skills.

If you are paying between two thousand and six thousand dollars to take a course at a college, shouldn't you be able to demand a teacher who speaks English at a college level of proficiency?

Actual Full-Time Professional Teaching Staff
[The dean's speech continues.]

In most colleges in the country, part-timers or graduate students teach the majority of classes. When full time (tenured, tenure track, and non-tenure track) professors teach undergraduate courses, they frequently teach in large lecture halls. At our college, our policy is in most classes to employ people whose full-time and only job and only passion is who teach you.

Summing Up the Differentiators
[The dean's speech continues.]

Ten to fifteen extra hands-on lab hours a week; class caps with no lecture halls; teachers that can actually speak the language and whose full-time passion is to teach. Without these, you risk increasing your odds of failure and the resulting financial loss and depression to as much as sixty percent or even greater.

Oh, About Your Scholarships...
[The dean's speech continues.]

(162)

You would think that this is the end of my lecture. I feel an obligation to be straight with all of you about another topic. If I did not speak about the fact that most of you will have your student aid and scholarships revoked, I might be guilty of lying by omission. Hold on to your seats. Some real "truth in advertising" is coming your way.

Colleges offer some degree of scholarship or a grant aid to almost everyone who applies to both state and private STEM programs. The aid makes families with stressed finances feel they can afford the education and from a psychological perspective, makes the applicant feel truly wanted by the college in question.

Remember my repeated observation that depending on the school, between forty and sixty percent of STEM students fail out within two years. I did not tell you about those who hang on with passing grades.

STEM students experience much tougher grading than Liberal Arts and Business students do. [36]

Take a look at the difference in Average Grade Point Average (GPA) as reported by PrepScholar.com:

Major	Average GPA
Education	3.36
Foreign Language	3.34
English	3.33
Music	3.30
Religion	3.22
Biology	3.02
Psychology	2.98
Economics	2.95
Engineering	2.90
Math	2.90
Chemistry	2.78

(49)

Keep in mind the Averages in the table, two thirds of merit scholarships at Tulane University are forfeited if the student's GPA falls below 2.7. One third are forfeited when the GPA falls below 3.0. Consider that the average GPA for a Chemistry major is a 2.78 and Math and Engineering majors are 2.9, that translates to almost half of those who did not fail out losing their scholarships. [138]

Perhaps you have been accepted at Wayne State University where most scholarships are lost when a student's GPA falls below either a 3.0, a 3.3 or a 3.5; [139] (or Auburn University, Louisiana State University, Stockton State University, the University of Central Florida or Arizona State University, where the scholarship retention floor is 3.0, [145] [140] [141] [142] [143])

If you think you can recover from one bad semester, it depends on the college. Auburn University's Scholarship Guidelines explicitly state that scholarship retentions (a) require at least a 3.0 cumulative, unadjusted Auburn GPA, (b) GPAs of 2.99 are not rounded to 3.0, and (c) scholarship reinstatement is not available even if the student achieves a 3.0 cumulative unadjusted GPA in a later term. [145]

(Not every college is so unfair. Texas A&M University does not cancel your scholarship until your GPA falls below a 2.0. [144] The University of Washington will place you on probation if your GPA falls below 2.0 and will allow you to average future semesters with better GPAs to retain your scholarship. [146])

A student who does not fail out and instead is still onboard even after seeing the majority of their peers fail out, may need to voluntarily withdraw anyway if the family finances truly depend on retaining student aid.

Most STEM students will have a tough first or second semester and lose their aid. This is why some colleges can award many times more in aid than they have money to give. **They do this because they know darn well that most of those scholarships will be cancelled within a few semesters as in some cases, only one scholarship in five will need to be paid in full.**

One more thing you need to know…

The Big Transferability Lie
[*The dean's speech continues.*]

(162)

Some schools with general accreditation do not have accredited Engineering, Healthcare, or Science programs. Instead, they represent that they have a "partnership" with another college that IS accredited for the STEM major of your interest. In their presentations, they will sell you on attending their "pre-engineering" or "pre-med" programs where their students can transfer to their partner school after two years and complete their STEM degree.

If you are considering such a program, I encourage you to tour the partner school. When you get to the "question and answer" session at the end of the presentation, just ask a simple question. Ask them how many transfer students from the first school they actually accepted in the current year. In many cases, the number will be so low as to be shocking.

There is a state college that we "partner" with. Last year, that college graduated about three hundred "pre-engineering," "pre-science," and "pre-med" students with associate degrees who then applied to transfer to our college. Out of the three hundred, we accepted twelve transfer students. Twelve! After all, we only have so much room for transfers.

Time for Truth in the Cost of College

Before I go, we need to discuss the true cost of college. Every parent I meet with budgets for a four-year adventure for their child's bachelor's degree. I already made clear that for probably eighty percent of you, your scholarships and other aid will be lost by the end of the second year if not the first.

For most of you, the true cost of your child's education is going to be higher. Much, much higher. In a study of 580 public four-year institutions, only 50 graduated the majority of their students in four years. [111] **For the mathematically challenged, that means less than nine percent earn their diploma in four years**. Even at many of the best, most prestigious universities that draw the best-qualified students, the four-year graduation rate is only thirty-six percent. [111]

If our nation truly had an effective "truth in advertising" law, we would call them "six-year schools" or even "six to eight years if you are lucky to graduate at all" schools.

Assuming your child makes it through to graduation, budgeting for five or six years of college is probably a more honest way of understanding the true cost of this adventure for most. Again, your five or six-year budget should assume the loss of your aid.

Is all of this scary and concerning? Sure it is. By facing these unpleasant facts, you can take steps to reduce horribly unpleasant surprises down the road.

(162)

With that, I encourage you to enjoy the tour of our new multi-million-dollar stadium!

[The dean's speech has ended.]

Dear reader, come back off the ledge. All is not lost. There are solutions and they are forthcoming in this book.

College Tour Checklist #1 – Questions to Ask – email to recruiter in advance

Name of School ➜ (Replace with the schools you are interested in.)	Rowan	Lafayette	Rutgers	Penn State	U of Arizona	Drexel
	1	2	3	4	5	6
Is the Major (not just the school regionally and professionally accredited?)						
Number of lecture hall courses in the first two years						
Maximum class size						
Number of students in this major who started four years ago.						
Number of students in this major who started four years ago who still are active in this major.						
Number of students in this major who started five years ago						
Number of students in this major who started five years ago who have graduated so far with a STEM B.S. degree						
Number of Google hits on RateMyProfessor.com for this school and "English Proficiency"						
Average hands-on weekly lab time for most students with this major						

Weeder Courses
and what to do about them

Let us start with a sanitized (edited) version of the Urban
Dictionary's definition of a "Weeder Course"

Weeder Class

A Weeder class is a class (typically in college) that is
characterized by having a large dropout rate due to rigorous
expectations, such as hard tests, impossible studying
requirements (15 hours a week or more), and excessive
homework. These classes "weed" out those who lack the
motivation to keep going or simply cannot take an abusive
workload anymore. Only the (really) hard working, gifted,
and borderline insane students make it through Weeder
classes.

Note: Weeder classes can seriously traumatize an individual,
destroy any ounce of confidence they have, and make them
seriously reconsider majors as most Weeder classes are
required.

Example sentence: At the beginning of the quarter the Intro to
Mechanical Engineering class had 70 students. By the end of
quarter, only 30 remained. That class is a Weeder class. If
you plan on taking this class, PREPARE FOR PAIN.

Some infamous Weeder classes: All calculus classes, physics,
chemistry, and engineering intro classes.

by Cochiloco April 07, 2014
http://www.urbandictionary.com/define.php?term=Weeder+Class

(123)

In 2012, a U.S. News and World Report article clearly exposed the toxic attitude of many teachers and administrators about their student-customers and Weeder courses.

According to the article, "Nearly half of all students who begin studying for a STEM degree switch majors, according to several studies. "Weed-out" classes, curve grading, and a lack of faculty involvement are to blame, experts said at a Bayer Corporation forum on STEM in higher education in Washington Wednesday." [137]

"We need to wash out the 'weed-them-out orientation' in the classroom," says Mary Fox, co-director at the Center for Study of Women, Science and Technology at Georgia Tech. "That is not a hospitable climate for students, we have to teach students to move along rather than have them sink or swim."
Many veteran STEM professors believe science should be hard, and the course work isn't something every student can do. For them, difficult freshman-year classes separate the cream of the crop. [137]

I see using tough courses to "Weed Out" potentially weaker students as a morally bankrupt approach to take tuition dollars in return for providing inadequate and/or incompetent education.

The school should be responsible for testing and otherwise determining that a student is qualified to take a course. They should then provide the level of competent education necessary for between 95% and 100% of the students to master all of the important topics within the course.

To those who believe in using courses to "weed out" the unfit, Weeders are a necessary and justified evil. To progressively minded people, Weeders are an unjustified abuse and fraud, which eventually results in delivering fewer qualified STEM graduates to society.

Strategies you can use to pass all of your courses, including the "Weeders," start on the next page.

A later chapter covers how schools can do a better job and increase pass rates north of ninety five percent without compromising on standards.

Schedule Stretching

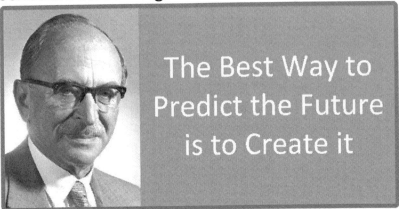

Image [155] Quotation from Dennis Gabor [156]

Let us start by examining the suggested freshman year curriculum that Rowan University presents to Mechanical Engineering Majors:

Mechanical Engineering Curriculum

Bold = minimum grade requirement of C-

FIRST YEAR			
FALL	**CR**	**SPRING**	**CR**
Freshman Engineering Clinic I (ENGR 01.101	2	Freshman Clinic 2 (ENGR 01.102)	2
Calculus I (MATH 01.130)	4	**Calculus II (MATH 01.131)**	4
Chemistry (CHEM06.100)	4	Introductory Mechanics I (PHYS 00.220)	4
Computer Sci. & Prog (CS 04.103)	4	Intro to Mechanical Design (ME10.101)*	3
General Education	3	College Composition I (COMP 01.111)	3
		* or Materials Science & Mfg. (ENGR 01.283)	
TOTAL	**17**	**TOTAL**	**16**

Chart from the Rowan University Website [129]

Here we have five courses per semester for the two freshman semesters. We already know that these courses taken together are so tough, that by the end of the first year, twenty to forty percent of freshman will have failed out and most of the remainder will be humiliated and will have lost their scholarships and financial aid.

We know that most students who do not fail completely generally take five to six years to graduate. (Some as STEM students; others in other majors.) It is reasonable to assume that they most will pass some courses and retake the courses they fail in a subsequent semester.

The key here is to stop the masochistic acceptance of the suggested calendar and negotiate a better one. The schedule above is a recipe for failure and depression. Twenty to thirty percent of freshmen will fail out their first year and another twenty to thirty percent will fail the next year. Financial aid loss will then depress many who remain.

As you will attend college before they have a chance to adopt the solutions in this book, you need to develop a strategy that (a) reduces your stress, (b) maintains your Grade Point Average, and (c) costs no more than true costs other families are paying over a six-year period.

Your road to success starts the summer before you start your "four-year" college. Investigate your lowest cost options for courses either on-line or at a community college. Line up a tutor because you should assume you will need one. Of the courses listed for Rowan's fall semester, it is doubtful that Clinic or Mechanical Design will be available. Find a Math Course and a Science Course. (Some community colleges have lower standards for some Liberal Arts courses, so skip the English unless you truly suck at this subject, and need remedial help.)

Yes, you will be poor, as the time to study for these two courses will eliminate most, if not all of your summer employment. As soon as possible, sit down with your advisor and evaluate these three approaches:

1. If the school permits inbound course transfers, try to get credit for those two courses ONLY if you are positive that the quality of those courses is as good as the four-year school. If the community college version of Calculus II will not prepare you for your four-year-school's required Calculus III course, you are better off repeating Calculus II in the fall. As you will already have mastered MOST of the course topics, your homework load and stress levels of the repeated course should be less.

2. If the school offers "Credit by Exam," try passing these two courses the week PRIOR to the start of class. (This way, if you fail, you can still take the courses in the fall.) Again, check with a teacher to be sure that the exam proves your competence for the next level course. Otherwise, repeat the course!

3. If for any reason, you do not transfer courses and you cannot pass them via an exam, the fall semester is absolutely the best time to take them. After all, you just spent your whole summer focusing on those topics.

4. Drop at least one other course you can take next summer. In this case, Composition I looks like a good choice as skipping any of the other courses may prevent you from taking courses you need in January.

Let us examine the possible outcomes of the above strategy:

1. If you got credit by transferring or obtaining credit by exams for two courses, your fall semester will be composed of only two courses assuming you postponed that English course until next summer.

2. In the best-case scenario, that means your fall semester will be composed of only two "Weeder" courses. In this scenario, you will have time to spend 10 to 15 hours per

week on homework for EACH course and still have time to relax on weekends. By focusing on two and only two courses, you have the best chance possible of a Grade Point Average high enough not to lose your college aid. You also maintain your self-esteem while the majority of your peers will either miserable because they were overwhelmed and failed out or because they passed, but not high enough to keep their aid.

3. Even if you wind up repeating both math and science courses in the fall, the fact that you spent the summer on them means those two fall courses should be of lower stress. Assuming you delay the English Comp class to the next summer, your freshman fall semester will be composed of only two tough courses and two lower-stress courses. This is not as positive an outcome as scenario number two. It is still dramatically better than if you accepted the program as presented to you by the college.

If you remember from a prior chapter that less than nine percent of STEM students graduate in four years, you can avoid a lot of pain and suffering by making better scheduling decisions up front. Remember that the largest issue is not class time. **It is the five to fifteen hours a week of time outside of class spent studying and on homework ON EACH COURSE that kills GPAs**.

Summer Schedule Warning

Many summer courses are on a "compressed" schedule of only four to eight weeks in duration. At many colleges, this is the ONLY option for summer semester courses. There are a number of possible explanations for this approach:

- If an elective course is less challenging and has less homework than a Weeder course, (i.e. Music

Appreciation instead of Calculus II,) then a four-to-eight-week schedule may be very doable.

- If you already passed this course at another college, your college may not accept the course for transfer credit. If this is the case, a compressed schedule for the purpose of a quick review and then exam for credit makes sense.

- Even if the class is a "Weeder" course, then a six or eight-week adventure might make sense under four conditions. First, this must be the ONLY course you are taking. Second, you are not working or vacationing during this time. Third, you commit to studying six to eight hours a day when not in class. Lastly, you either engage a tutor or study group available at LEAST every other day.

Some online summer courses can extend through the entire summer.

If your prospective college only offers compressed schedule summer courses and limits the courses you may transfer from other colleges, it may make sense to look elsewhere.

This may be ok for a course that is not all that challenging, but a disaster for Weeder courses.

Customizing Your Own Education

Many colleges are inflexible when considering the material in this section. Some will charge less tuition for students they reclassify as "part time" or "non-matriculated" statuses. However, many colleges later become inflexible and will penalize students with these classifications. They may, and then give these students low priority in signing up for some courses while also giving them a hard time about matriculating later on. As in many other areas in life, "buyer beware."

Take a moment to focus on the following chart. The traditional STEM program typically requires five courses each Fall semester and five courses each Winter semester and results in the 40% to 60% failure rate and five or six years of school for those who do not fail. [147]

Planning Your Bachelor's Degree – Courses Per Semester						
Option "0": The old way (with 40% to 60% STEM failure)						
Semester		Option				
		"0"				
Year 1	Summer					
	Fall	5				
	Winter	5				
	Summer					
Year 2	Fall	5				
	Winter	5				
	Summer					
Year 3	Fall	5				
	Winter	5				
	Summer					
Year 4	Fall	5				
	Winter	5				
	Summer					
Year 5	Fall					
	Winter					
	Summer					
Year 6	Fall					
	Winter					
	Summer					
Total Courses Taken		40				

Option 1. You still graduate in four years!

One part of the solution may be to utilize summers for classes instead of jobs, internships, and play. Here is a schedule where:

- The summer after high school, you take one and only one course to lighten the load on your freshman fall semester where traditionally there are so many failures.

- Each of the following summers, you take two courses. This lowers your fall and winter semester course and homework loads by 20%.

- One net effect of the schedule is that the student only takes three courses in the fall of their first year.

- The other net effect of the schedule is that the student never takes more than four courses in any other semester.

- More than other options you will read about, the colleges that will serve you best will offer the flexibility to pursue this approach without financial penalties.

Approach Drawbacks

This approach works best when an internship is not required by the school and the student can manage to get through college without working (or working much) during their summers.

The approach also recognizes that some students will feel deprived without their summers off, as some will want more down time.

Note that some colleges will charge you full-time tuition for fall and winter, even with a lightened course load and then charge you even more to take the summer classes.

Planning Your Bachelor's Degree – Courses Per Semester						
Option "0": The old way						
Option 1: 4 years						
Semester		Option				
		"0"	1			
Year 1	Summer		1			
	Fall	5	3			
	Winter	5	4			
	Summer		2			
Year 2	Fall	5	4			
	Winter	5	4			
	Summer		2			
Year 3	Fall	5	4			
	Winter	5	4			
	Summer		2			
Year 4	Fall	5	4			
	Winter	5	4			
	Summer		2			
Year 5	Fall					
	Winter					
	Summer					
Year 6	Fall					
	Winter					
	Summer					
Total Courses Taken		40	40			

There are also some more enlightened colleges will charge you full-time for fall and winter, but then not charge at all for the summer courses.

If you want to pursue any of these "better" options when selecting your college, you will need to be an inquisitive and demanding consumer. Taking their recipe for course loads is a proven recipe to fail 40% to 60% of their customers.

Option 2. Face Reality / Minimize Stress

Most STEM students who graduate do so in five years anyway. My suggestion is that you consider lowering your stress by spreading out your course loads before you fail and are discouraged.

Planning Your Bachelor's Degree – Courses Per Semester					
Option "0": The old way. Option 1: 4 years.					
Option 2: 5 years.					
Semester		Option			
		"0"	1	2	
Year 1	Summer		1	1	
	Fall	5	3	2	
	Winter	5	4	3	
	Summer		2	2	
Year 2	Fall	5	4	3	
	Winter	5	4	3	
	Summer		2	2	
Year 3	Fall	5	4	3	
	Winter	5	4	3	
	Summer		2	2	
Year 4	Fall	5	4	3	
	Winter	5	4	3	
	Summer		2	2	
Year 5	Fall			3	
	Winter			3	
	Summer			2	
Year 6	Fall				
	Winter				
	Summer				
Total Courses Taken		40	40	40	

Option Two takes the approach in Option 1 and spreads out your schedule year-round over five years. You never take more than three courses in any semester and so never have more than thirty hours a week of homework!

This may be the best of the options. It balances the need to lower your failure risk with the desire to successfully graduate and get you into the job market as soon as possible.

Drawbacks of this approach

The drawbacks of this approach are the same as Option 1, but spread out into five years.

Some colleges will require you to pay full price for each of the five years, even though you are taking less than ten courses per year.

This is their way of perpetuating the system where the odds are that you will fail and lose your financial aid.

If this schedule works for you and a prospective college will not work with you, it may be time to consider attending elsewhere.

Option 3 – Easy does it

The majority of STEM students in four-year baccalaureate programs who graduate do so in five or six years. They are students who got good grades in high school, generally graduated in the top percentiles of their class, and scored well on their SAT exams. Even so, less than nine percent will graduate in four years.

Why not "test the waters" by choosing a college that allows your first year of study to be only two courses per semester (plus one in the summer prior to your freshman fall semester).

If the workload seems manageable and your grades are "As," then you can switch to taking more courses and a five-year trajectory.

However, if you are getting Bs or Cs when taking two courses a semester, then stay the course. There is nothing costlier than failure.

For most students, I recommend they consider Option 2. Thirty hours a week of homework (from three STEM courses) is tough, but manageable for most. By getting into the job market after five years of school, you gain the income from that year to help pay off college debts and launch your career.

For students who need to work at least part time through college, planning on a six-year adventure where the school bills only for the courses taken makes sense.

You will need to work with a progressively minded school who values your success over their immediate income.

Planning Your Bachelor's Degree – Courses Per Semester					
Option "0": The old way. Option 1: 4 years. Option 2: 5 years. Option 3: 6 years.					
Semester		Option			
		"0"	1	2	3
Year 1	Summer		1	1	1
	Fall	5	3	2	2
	Winter	5	4	3	2
	Summer		2	2	2
Year 2	Fall	5	4	3	2
	Winter	5	4	3	2
	Summer		2	2	2
Year 3	Fall	5	4	3	2
	Winter	5	4	3	2
	Summer		2	2	3
Year 4	Fall	5	4	3	2
	Winter	5	4	3	3
	Summer		2	2	2
Year 5	Fall			3	2
	Winter			3	3
	Summer			2	2
Year 6	Fall				2
	Winter				2
	Summer				2
Total Courses Taken		40	40	40	40

Option 4 – Winter is harder, but summers off

Suppose you are in a program where summer internships are required or you absolutely need to work summers in order to get the cash you need to live.

Assuming that thirty hours a week of homework is most you can sustain over a long period of time, a college that bills only for the courses taken is required so you can successfully graduate with your sanity preserved in six years.

In addition, if you need to work part time, nine or ten hours of class per week with fifteen to thirty hours of homework is possible for some people, especially while young and single.

As with the other options, you will need to find a college that will work with you and not financially penalize you for taking steps to insure your success. (My experience and research show that most are NOT flexible.)

The Career Threatening Weeder Course

As previously mentioned, I spent most of seventh and eighth grade in bed or on crutches due to a genetic disorder. I entered high school not having math since sixth grade. The lack of math background, combined with both pain and many painkillers, meant high school math was mostly a disastrous series of failures for me. I convinced myself that I sucked at math and avoided math courses in college.

Prior to the age of fifty, I experienced two panic attacks. The first one occurred during an exam in an advanced programming course where the test included a problem requiring knowledge of algebra and trig that I just did not have.

Planning Your Bachelor's Degree – Courses Per Semester					
Option "0": The old way. One: 1: 4yrs. Two: 5yrs. Three: 6yrs. Option 4: 6 years but no summers.					
Semester		Option			
		"0"	1	2	3	
Year 1	Summer		1	1	1	
	Fall	5	3	2	2	3
	Winter	5	4	3	2	3
Year 2	Summer		2	2	2	
	Fall	5	4	3	2	3
	Winter	5	4	3	2	3
Year 3	Summer		2	2	2	
	Fall	5	4	3	2	3
	Winter	5	4	3	2	3
Year 4	Summer		2	2	3	
	Fall	5	4	3	2	3
	Winter	5	4	3	3	3
Year 5	Summer		2	2	2	
	Fall			3	2	4
	Winter			3	3	4
Year 6	Summer			2	2	
	Fall				2	4
	Winter				2	4
	Summer				2	
Total Courses Taken		40	40	40	40	40

The second attack was during a Geology exam where again, an exam problem required math knowledge that I just did not have.

Rationally, I should have just skipped those problems, as I would still have earned an A or a B by correctly answering all of the other ones. However, the mind is a funny thing. Running into those small challenges somehow surfaced all of my irrational fears of being unworthy, of being stupid, and that my deficiencies in math would someday sabotage by career.

(Despite those setbacks, I did earn an "A" or "B" in those courses.)

When it came time to apply to graduate with a bachelor's degree, my lack of an approved math course stood in my way. My wife could not understand the degree of my distress. She pointed out that due to work requirements as a programmer and database administrator, I had purchased and mastered one college textbook on algorithms and another on statistics. I used math in my job every day and actually enjoyed it. By this time in my career, I had programmed in a half-dozen computer languages and more than a dozen databases. In addition, there was some math in each of my half dozen computer science courses.

However, I had not had what in my mind was a "real" math course.

With great fear, I planned to face my math demon. In the fall of 1992, I notified my employer that I needed to cut back my hours from my normal fifty hours a week to forty hours a week for the entire semester. As my wife had earned "A's" in all of her college math courses, she became my tutor. I made a written schedule that included three hours each night to study and four hours each Saturday and each Sunday. I took no other college courses that semester.

I would not take any road trips to see friends or take any vacation that semester. I was determined and committed and still scared to death.

The evening class began. The teacher would assign the "odd" numbered problems. I would do them all. When a concept stumped me and my wife's explanation made no sense, I got on the phone with friends. The teacher even skipped some chapters and fearing that I would miss something, I read them and did every problem in every chapter.

I bought another math textbook that was supposed to explain things more clearly. If a topic in my school-assigned book was fuzzy, I would read the explanations in the competing books and work on those problems as well.

The professor did not believe in grading on a "curve," even though a number of classmates were failing the course. However, students could earn up to five extra points by doing some additional assignments based on worksheets handed out as extra credit each week.

I finished the course with a grade of 105. (Five extra points were awarded for doing extra assignments.) My transcript only says "A." What it should have said was "Math Demon: Dead and Buried."

You may discover you have your own personal demon. Calculus? Organic Chemistry? Trig and Algebra? Latin? Do not let it ruin your life. See if you can take a semester with only the Weeder course or perhaps the Weeder course and a course in art or music or something else with minimal homework. Queue up a tutor. Know that alternate explanations for most STEM topics are available online, often on Youtube.com. Tutors who are inexpensive, competent, and who speak your native language, can be found online and can provide help via Skype or any other video conference method.

Buyer Beware, Be Brave, and Prepare to Say NO!

Most colleges will not work with you. They may require you to take exactly their schedule of courses exactly on the semesters of their choosing.

Prior to accepting an offer to attend, sit down with your advisor and review your personal education strategy with them.

If the college is too rigid, then consider going elsewhere no matter how attractive the student lounge or the phony student aid package.

But isn't "schedule stretching" expensive?

Not when compared to the cost of failing. Failing and restarting is expensive. Seven years to get a Bachelor's degree with a loss of student aid is expensive. Therapy for damaged self-esteem is expensive. Without lowering standards, you can take steps to be in the twenty percent of students who graduate with their psyches intact in four to five years.

By using relatively inexpensive community colleges and online schools to prepare, you improve your odds of actually graduating in four to five years as opposed to six to eight years or not at all.

Preemptive Tutoring
Otherwise known as "tutoring, you've been doing this all wrong."

(162)

Consider how tutoring works for most college students.

Without any expectation that tutoring is, the typical student registers for a class with the expectation that they are qualified to take the course. After all, most people assume it is the college's responsibility to determine the prerequisite knowledge required prior to allowing the student to register for a course.

As an extreme and somewhat silly example, a reasonable person would expect that no college anywhere would permit a freshman to take a course where they actually perform brain surgery. Using the same rationale, any college who offers a course where more than ten percent of previous course takers failed, should see that happening as a cause for alarm and take actions the book will explain in a future chapter. However, the combination of "Weeder" courses and crazy workloads translate to the expectation by the student that they just need to focus and do their best.

In this example, the student registers for the class and then decided to work as hard as they can and hope for the best.

After subtracting for holidays, most college courses have a duration of about 14 weeks and so that will be the length used for this illustration.

During the typical first class, the teacher confirms the exact textbook needed and presents the first lecture.

Very often, the first one to three weeks are reviews of material that should have been mastered in the prerequisite courses. If there are quizzes during this time, there may or may not be new and more difficult material to master.

By the third week, the teacher is presents new material at a rapid pace. If this is a course with weekly quizzes, week three or four will include a poor score on one or two consecutive quizzes. By now, an intelligent and conscientious student will go running to the college's tutoring center where they may or may not get someone actually qualified to be a tutor.

Tutoring is teaching. Just because a college senior got a high grade in Advanced Calculus and understands all the Concepts in Advanced Calculus, does not mean that they have the skills to teach any of those concepts.

Teachers often reserve the middle week of a course for midterm preparation and presentation. They often reserve the last week of a course for final exams and exam preparation. Thus, new material in most Weeder courses is presented in only ten weeks.

The student in need of help may or may not get a competent tutor. Even if they do, the tutoring may not be available on as many hours or days sufficient to get the student caught up with the class. After all, while the tutoring focuses on current deficiencies, the class is marching ahead and consuming one tenth of the course knowledge each week.

Unfortunately, community colleges do not offer many of the Weeder courses (such as Engineering Technology). In this case, the strategy of taking the course early is not available.

So, depending on the college, between forty percent and sixty percent of the intelligent and hardworking students who did well in high school and took all the prerequisite courses the college requires, will actually start behind, rarely catch up, and either fail or be demoralized with a low grade if they pass.

Yet, tutoring is one of the stock answers given by teachers and advisors when a struggling student raises their hand and says, "I need help."

A STEM degree can translate to lifetime earnings of between three and four million dollars. Failing to graduate can saddle the student with a lifetime of debt, poor credit, and damaged self-esteem. Failing any course, including a Weeder course, is not an acceptable outcome.

Assuming you have already pushed one or two courses to a summer program, there will be at least one Weeder course awaiting you each semester.

This is where online tutors, and tutorial services, come into the educational picture.

With very few questions posted online to upperclassmen and alumni, we absolutely know which courses we are taking are likely to be Weeder courses.

There are also, what I call the "Personal Weeders." Here is an example from my family. When my older son first went to college, it was with the intention of majoring in Electrical Engineering. He is very mathematically oriented. Subjects like Advanced Calculus pose no threat to him. However, for him, college-level English Composition was a nightmare. He took the course in Community College the summer prior to entering his four-year college and STILL he struggled that fall with that course at the four-year school while breezing through the technical courses. The moral here is to be self-aware and not just take the advice of strangers about which courses are likely to be the challengers for you personally.

With open eyes, you have identified those courses this semester that are likely to be your personal Weeders. Getting a grade below a "B" in any of them is not an option. Know in advance that depending on the curving practices of the teacher and college, that it is possible that less than ten percent of your peers will score a "B" or higher.

This is your notice that just working hard and studying with your peers is probably not good enough.

Nepal's Mount Everest is the tallest mountain on earth. Climbing Mount Everest is a challenging and dangerous adventure. Blinding sub-zero temperature storms of snow and sleet can happen at almost any time. Avalanches happen with little warning. The fatality rate of those climbing Mount Everest is almost two percent. (Exactly 1.8% for those at home keeping score.)

Knowledgeable mountain climbers who have many years of experience climbing other mountains would not typically think of climbing Mount Everest without Nepal's famed "Sherpa Guides" with them during their adventure.

The Sherpas are not just locals; they are highly trained and highly skilled Professional Guides. A Professional Guide is not just someone who is an expert climber. A Professional Guide is an expert climber who is able to help other climbers stay alive and then reach their goal.

When I say "during their adventure," I mean the Sherpas educate the climbers before the day of the climb. I mean the Sherpas are within sight of the climbers on the first steps of the climb. I mean the Sherpas are physically with the climbers every hour of every day going up and then every hour of every day coming down.

The presence of the Sherpas does not guarantee success. There have been multiple trips accompanied by Sherpas, where disaster has struck and fatalities happened anyway. As the thinking goes, the expense of the Sherpas at least improves the odds that the climber will succeed in their goal.

Considering the failure rate among Weeder courses, I suggest you strongly consider the risk reduction associated with hiring your own Professional Sherpa IN ADVANCE OF THE START OF YOUR COURSE to act as your guide day-by-day and week-by-week during the course. If after the midterm, you have a Grade Point Average of 95% or better, you can probably stop paying for the tutor and complete the course on your own.

Consider the financial and emotional costs of doing poorly in your Weeder course. A Professional Tutor with the right course knowledge, who also has the proper teaching skills, who is available for the hours and days your required for you to get your "A," can help you graduate on time, with your financial aid intact, and on your way to career earnings of between three and four million dollars.

Tutor Selection

Your college's free tutoring is probably a risky proposition where already behind and stressed, you must accept whatever resource is offered, despite their suitability and availability to meet your needs. However, there are better paths to selecting not just a tutor, but also your very own Sherpa.

Assume you have already done what you can do to lower your course load, and also to lower your stress. You took certain courses online or at community college. There are certain courses (such as Engineering Technology) that your college may require taken at the college. It is time to find your Sherpa.

Just as the most successful companies fill open jobs by selecting the most suitable person after considering multiple candidates, you should interview multiple tutors and be in a position to select the person best suited to help you.

The tutor selection process starts as soon as you have registered for your courses. Hopefully, this is at LEAST three to four weeks before the start of the semester. Your process should include the following steps:

1. Identify Tutor Sources
2. Identify Potential Tutors
3. Interview and Grade Potential Tutors
4. Choose Your Primary and Secondary Tutors
5. Tutor Daily Until They Are Not Needed
6. Evaluate if a Tutor Change is warranted

1. Identify Tutor Sources

There are multiple ways to look out for potential Tutors. Most colleges have a Tutoring Center. Many, if not most college counselors and teachers have a file of tutors they have referred students to in the past. There are both physical and online billboards at every college. There is always Craig's List. A Google search "sources for college tutors" will present you with both paid ads and non-paid results.

Your goal is to search out and interview as many tutoring candidates as needed in order to arrive at three outstanding finalists. You may need to interview four people or you may need to interview a dozen. If this seems like a bother, just remember that your career, your income, and your self-esteem may hang on your choosing the best person for the job.

2. Identify Potential Tutors

As you email or message potential tutors, you may want to find out a few things before taking the time for a telephone or in-person interview. Some questions you may want answered in advance at a very high level:

a. What they charge
b. How well they know the subject
c. Whether they know how the subject is taught at your college

3. Interview and Grade Potential Tutors

Once you have decided that a potential tutor is worth interviewing, invite them to join you for a beverage. (Unless this will be a Skype-only relationship.)

Now is the time to engage in a conversation that covers six topics in depth. All you need to do is ask the following questions and TAKE NOTES!

a. What is the tutor's general knowledge of the subject?

b. What does the tutor know, about how your school teaches this subject?

c. What is their teaching experience? (Just because someone knows about a topic does not mean they are any good at teaching others.)

d. Are they available to tutor an hour a day Monday through Friday if needed?

e. Are they available to tutor more times the week before midterms and finals?

f. Will they provide you references and contact information for those references?

g. What is their hourly rate? Will they offer a lower rate if you commit to a certain number of hours?

h. How well do they speak English?

i. If they are a student, what is their course load?

j. If they teach, what is their course load?

k. If they tutor others, how many?

l. What is their geographic availability, transportation availability, or ability to tutor over Skype (or Viber or ooVoo or Google Hangouts, or whatever).

m. Are they willing to tutor you with another classmate to reduce costs?

During the conversation, consider giving them a grade in each
of the following areas:

Tutor Interview Chart				
	1	2	3	4
Name	Bill Smith	Ahmed M.	Sara Jones	Fran J.
Email	bs@123.edu	am@123.edu	SJ@456.com	FrJ@rrr.com
Phone	555-555-1212	555-555-1212	555-555-1212	555-555-1212
$/hour	20	30	25	15
1. General Subject Matter knowledge	A	B	A	A
2. This school's course knowledge	A	A	A	F
3. Ability to teach	A	A	A	A
4. Available at least one hour per day Monday through Friday?	A	A	A	A
5. Weeks not available this semester	1	1	0	0
6. Vetted through service?	no	no	Yes	Yes
7. Vetted through Rate My Professor.com?	A	B	C	F
8. Vetted through Rate my Teacher.com?				
9. Recommended by whom?	3 references			
10. Extra availability the week prior to midterms and finals?	yes	yes	yes	Yes

In the example above, the feedback on RateMyProfessor.com
narrowed down the list to three good choices.

4. Choose your Primary and Secondary Tutors

As Tutors are real people, they come with the same risks as the rest of us. People get sick and their loved ones get sick. People unexpectedly change jobs or move. People disappear. (Really!) The biggest risk is a terrible reality. Some people who interview really well for a job turn out to be a major disappointment once they are actually past the initial "honeymoon period."

As a result, be sure to let one or two of your candidates know that they were a very close fit and you will keep them in mind in case the tutor you select does not work out.

5. Tutor Daily Until Not Needed

Do not wait to fall behind. If the first few weeks of class are easy, just meet with your tutor once or twice a week during that time. If things start to get unbearable in week three, four, or five, then ramp up to as many days a week as you need to get your "A."

Most students will not have the money for tutoring by separate tutors in every course, so it is important to select a tutor who is generally strong where you are not.

If you are in a course with a weekly quiz and a midterm, and you ace every one of these with a high "A," then it is probably an OK decision to stop the tutoring for the remainder of this course IF and only IF it appears you are absorbing the information well enough on your own.

6. Evaluate if a Tutor Change is Warranted

If at ANY TIME during the course, you are falling behind and the tutor is not helping you turn things around, there is a hard decision to make. MAKE IT! Someone who is a perfectly good tutor for someone else may just not understand your learning style.

Your college career, your future income, and your psychological well-being are too important to accept course failure because you "felt bad" about changing Tutors.

After the course is over, think back and evaluate the degree to which your tutor helped you raise your grade. Perhaps you will determine you do not need a tutor for the follow-on course. Perhaps you will. Perhaps you will decide you do, but need someone else. This is your life. I am just giving you options.

Transfer Courses and Credit by Exam
Sometimes, But Only Sometimes, a Good Idea

By now, you understand that your challenge is to pass forty courses with a high enough Grade Point Average (GPA) that you maintain your college aid while obtaining your diploma in approximately four and one-half years. (I am including all of your summers, including the summer prior to your first year and the summer after your senior year.)

I have already noted that taking courses outside of your four-year college is one way to prepare for an easier way to take the course and insure a higher GPA.

There are three alternate options to consider as part of taking these outside courses.

- Course Transfer
- Credit by Exam
- Course Waiver

If you take a course outside of your primary college, the college may or may not accept that course for transfer. Transfer means that you have that many fewer credits required for your diploma. The grade earned for a transferred course is NOT considered when calculating your GPA at most colleges. (This is actually the case at all colleges that I am aware of.) Course Transfer can be a good idea, or a terrible mistake.

The Financial Impact

Assuming your course cost at the outside institution was lower than what your college charges, this approach may reduce your overall college cost. However, this benefit is partially offset as some colleges charge an "evaluation fee" before accepting an outside course for credit.

The GPA Impact

If this is a course you are convinced is a Weeder you will struggle in no matter what, (for some, Organic Chemistry is such an example), taking it outside of your college insures that your low-but-passing grade will not lower your overall GPA.

However, if retaking the course at your four-year school is likely to result in raising your GPA and preserving your aid, taking transfer credit could be the tipping point as other courses lower your GPA and cost you financially.

The Poor Foundation Theory

Really understanding some courses (such as Calculus I) gives you the foundation to lessen your struggles in subsequent courses (such as Calculus II, II, and IV). If your external school did not teach the course as thoroughly as your four-year school, the short-term benefit could be canceled out by struggle and failure in the subsequent courses.

The Bottom Line

There is no one easy answer that applies to everyone when it comes to transferring courses. By considering the above topics, you will be able to make the right decision for your situation.

Credit by Exam

Assume you took that course online or at a community college and mastered the content. After considering the implications pro and con, you decide that you want credit for taking that course. You visit your advisor and learn that for whatever reason, the school will not accept transfer credit for that course.

For many schools and subjects, you can arrange to earn those credits by taking a single exam while the subject matter is still relatively fresh in your brain.

All of the same concerns listed in the previous section apply.

In most cases, your passing grade in the Credit by Exam process reduces the number of credits you need for that Bachelor's degree but does not affect your GPA one way or another.

But in some colleges, credit by exam does not count toward calculating your GPA while in others it certainly does. Another discussion with your advisor is in order.

I listed the Thomas Edison University TECEP program below just as an example. Your college may offer its own version and/or accept exams from the national CLEP - College-Level Examination Program and/or DSST Exams (formerly DANTES).

From the Thomas Edison University website:
TECEP® Thomas Edison Credit by Exam Program

Computer Concepts & Applications	English Composition I
Security Analysis & Portfolio Mgmt	English Composition II
Financial Institutions & Markets	Public Relations
Managerial Communications	Technical Writing
Marketing Communications	Environmental Ethics
Principles of Financial Acctng	Intro to News Reporting
Prin. of Managerial Acctng	Music History II
World History 1600 to Present	Intro to Critical Reasoning
Introduction to Political Science	Microeconomics
Intro to Comparative Politics	Abnormal Psychology
Psychology of Women	Introduction to Sociology
Negotiations & Conflict Mgmt	Marriage & the Family
Business in Society	The Science of Nutrition
Strategic Mgmt	Applied Liberal Arts Math
Sales Mgmt	College Algebra
Advertising	Prin. of Statistics
Operations Mgmt	Federal Income Taxation
Network Technology	Medical Terminology
	Radiation Safety Officer

From the Thomas Edison University website:

CLEP - College-Level Examination Program

Thomas Edison State University awards credit for CLEP examinations, which have been reviewed and recommended for college credit by the American Council on Education (ACE) for specific exhibit dates.

Prior to registering ... refer to the current CLEP website to confirm that the examination ... is still active: www.collegeboard.com/clep.

Current college-level examinations in the College-Level Examination Program (CLEP) are administered at Thomas Edison State University in Trenton, N.J., once a month. Students may request the registration form from the Office of Test Administration at (609) 984-1181. Students who want to test at another location or want more detailed information on the examinations and study materials may contact: CLEP. P.O. Box 6600. Princeton, NJ 08541-6600. (800) 257-9558 www.collegeboard.com/clep

To send reports sent to TESU, enter college code, 2748, at the time of testing.

A sample of available CLEP courses:
Eng Comp I, ENC-102 Eng Comp II (6 Cr), Eng Comp I, (3 Cr), Genl Math I, MAT-103, Genl Math II (6 Cr), Coll Algebra (3 Cr), MAT-129 PreCalc (3 Cr), MAT-231 Calc I (4 Cr), Intro to Sociology (3 Cr), Amer Lit I AND LIT-206, Amer Lit II (6 Cr), Analysis & Interpretation of Lit AND LIT-292, Analysis & Interpretation of Lit II (6 Cr), Eng Lit AND LIT-209 Eng Lit II (6 Cr)
Intro French I, FRE-102, Intro French II, FRE-201, Intermediate French (6 or 9 Cr), Intro German I, GRM-102, Intro German II, GRM-201, Intermediate German (6 or 9 Cr), Intro Hum II: Poetry, Drama and NarrAND HUS-103, Intro to Humanities III: Music (6 Cr), Intro Spanish I, SPA-102 Intro Spanish II, SPA-201 Intermediate Spanish (6 or 9 Cr), Amer Government (3 Cr), Amer Hist I (3 Cr), HIS-114 Amer Hist II (3 Cr), Dev. Psych (3 Cr), PSY-230 Intro to Educational Psych (3 Cr), Intro to Psychology (3 Cr), SOC-101 Intro to Sociology (3 Cr), Macroecon (3 Cr), ECO-112 Microecon (3 Cr), Social Sci & Hist I, SOS-102 Social Sci & Hist II (6 Cr), Western Civ I (3 Cr), HIS-102 Western Civ II (3 Cr) , Genl Biology I, BIO-112 Genl Biology II (6 Cr) , Calc I (4 Cr), CHE-111 Genl Chemistry I, CHE-112 Genl Chemistry II (6 Cr), Coll Algebra (3 Cr), MAT-102, Genl Math I, MAT-103, Genl Math II (6 Cr), Natural Sci I, NAS-102 Natural Sci II (6 Cr), PreCalc (3 Cr), ACC-101 Principles of Financial Acctng (3 Cr) Intro to Computers (3 Cr), LAW-201 Business Law (3 Cr) Principles of Mgmt (3 Cr), MAR-301 Principles of Marketing (3 Cr)

DSST Exams (formerly DANTES)

Please note that Thomas Edison State University awards credit for DSST examinations which have been reviewed and recommended for credit by the American Council on Education (ACE) for specific exhibit dates. Students who want more detailed information on the DSST program and

study materials may contact:
Prometric, DSST Program. 2000 Lenox Drive, 3rd floor
Lawrenceville, NJ 08648. Toll free (877) 471-9860
www.getcollegecredit.com

Some DSST courses:

Business Ethics and Society
Business Mathematics
Environment and Humanity
Human Resource Management

Principles of Physical Science I
Introduction to Business
Introduction to Computing
Management Information Systems
Organizational Behavior
A History of the Vietnam War
Personal Finance
Fundamentals of College Algebra

Principles of Statistics
Fundamentals of Cybersecurity
Technical Writing

Art of the Western World
Principles of Finance
The Civil War and Reconstruction
Principles of Supervision
Criminal Justice
Foundations of Education
Fundamentals of Counseling
General Anthropology
Human/Cultural Geography
Ethics in America
Introduction to Law Enforcement
Introduction to World Religions
Lifespan Developmental Psychology
Principles of Public Speaking
Rise and Fall of the Soviet Union
Substance Abuse

From the Thomas Edison University Website [11]

Course Waiver by Exam

Some colleges will allow you to take an exam to waive taking a
required course, but will not give you any credit for doing so.
The only reason I can think of to pursue this path is if you need
to open a slot to take an additional elective course to satisfy the
requirement of a second major or a minor. Otherwise, if you do
not get credit, why bother?

Online Courses
The good, the bad, and the ugly

Online courses have matured from highly suspicious to a vast array of credit and non-credit ways to learn. Their cost ranges from free to very expensive; and the quality ranges from poor to wonderful.

Time for me to rant and blow off a little steam….

The Massachusetts Institute of Technology is arguably one of the finest STEM schools on planet earth. They have placed all the course materials from virtually all of their courses online at http://ocw.mit.edu/courses/.

Unfortunately, I am not aware that any regionally and professionally accredited institution that has a way for students to study the MIT materials, possibly work with a tutor, take an exam, and then be awarded credit.

(There are three colleges praised later in the book who offer exams for a tiny percentage of these courses. It is time for these or other colleges to dramatically expand the number of exams they offer. That topic is covered in depth later in the book.)

Knowledge for knowledge's sake is fine, but I am trying to get you a legitimate degree that employers will accept to launch a well-compensated career.

If you become aware of any such program or institution that leverages either MIT or other public resources, please contact me at **www.thestemstudentsurvivalguide.com/feedback** so

I can update my website and future editions of this book.

Some online courses include teachers, tests, and deadlines while at the other extreme, there are online courses with no human interaction other than the student with no deadlines whatsoever.

When considering whether to take an online course, one needs to be very honest with themselves as to the degree of discipline they have. The more flexibility and freedom from assignments and deadlines one has, the more of an opportunity for the evil demon called Procrastination has to sabotage your success.

With that said, my thanks to Susan Brown at http://www.learningonlineblog.com/2014/03/22/websites-teaching-calculus/
who in 2014 gathered the following online resources for teaching calculus (and other courses). I provide this only as evidence that with a little Google searching, most college courses are available in some form online.

Khan Academy: https://www.khanacademy.org/
Thousands of topics taught at every level.

MIT Open Course Ware: http://ocw.mit.edu/index.htm
MIT OpenCourseWare (OCW) is a web-based publication of virtually all MIT course content. OCW is open and available to the world and is a permanent MIT activity. The site includes more than 1,000 courses.

Mooculus: https://mooculus.osu.edu/ A site just for Calculus

Coursera: https://www.coursera.org/
Hundreds of Specializations and courses in business, computer science, data science from many leading universities including Penn, Johns Hopkins, University of Michigan, Stanford, UCSanDiego, and Duke. (As of the writing of this text, Coursera was migrating from a free platform to a paid platform.)

Calculus-help: http://www.calculus-help.com/ The focus is on Calculus

S.O.S. Mathematics. http://www.sosmath.com/
S.O.S. MATHematics is a free resource for math review material from
Algebra to Differential Equations.

From Susan Brown's Web Page [132]

Stuck on one specific homework assignment? Consider making
your first stop YouTube.com.

Weeder Failure Recovery

Joe (not his real name) is one of my son Jerry's classmates. A dual chemistry / biology major, Joe is required to take and pass Calculus I, Calculus II, and Calculus III.

As of this writing, Joe has failed Calculus II three times in three consecutive semesters.

As Albert Einstein defined it, insanity is "doing the same thing over and over again and expecting different results." [39]

Assuming Joe is paying attention in class, doing his homework the best he can, asking others for help, and getting the proper amount of sleep, a different approach is called for if Joe is to ever pass the course.

Even a single failure should be treated as a potential symptom of something serious and career threatening. Let us spend some time and figure out what should be done for Joe to master the course material.

Your high school classes should have already ingrained the Scientific Method into your brains. By treating a course failure as we would a failed experiment, we should first perform a "root cause analysis." Let us take some time to speculate (hypothesize) what could be causing these failures and what to do to achieve success.

In this case, start by assuming all the assumptions in the text about studiousness and sleep above are correct. Here are possible other root cause reasons that Joe keeps failing Calculus II:

1. Prerequisite knowledge

In STEM programs, courses tend to build on subject matter taught in prior courses. It does no good to give a passing grade to someone who scored 70% or 80% on their exams if the missing 20% or 30% of knowledge will cause them to fail a future course. This issue alone is one where "grading on a curve" makes no sense. If the majority of the students are scoring 50% on the exams, (Not a curve,) then a free remedial class is called for.

(Free because the college should take the responsibility through pre-test or other method of qualifying the student before allowing them to register for the course. After passing the pre-requisite, the second attempt at the failed course should also be free.)

If Joe passed Pre-Calculus or Calculus I with less than total subject mastery, he may have failed to fully learn certain concepts essential for understanding Calculus II. Repeating Calculus II over and over may neither identify Joe's knowledge gaps nor fill them.

As soon as Joe (or anyone) fails a course, the very question to ask is if Joe has any gaps in his prerequisite course knowledge.

One option is to give Joe a comprehensive exam that covers all of the content from Calculus I plus all of the content from the Calculus I prerequisite course. While this book advocates doing this prior to each course, it should certainly be done the moment Joe fails a test during the semester.

Joe should be given detailed results of the exam. Depending what is missing, tutoring in the gaps, or even repeating a lower level course might make more sense than immediately repeating a failed course.

Joe should not take the Calculus II course again until he is certain that 100% of all prerequisite topics have been mastered.

2. Teacher competence

A teacher might be an expert in the field they are teaching. They might even be famous for their research and/or discoveries and/or inventions. However, like a tutor, none of those attributes guaranty that a teacher is a competent instructor. If that teacher's explanations do not educate the student, then the student needs to find a better teacher, even if that means taking the course at a different college or taking the course with a private or small group tutor and then taking an exam to earn their credit.

Joe is the consumer (purchaser) of the education. If the school provides an inferior service, then it is up to Joe to find a different source to help him develop the necessary knowledge and related skills.

3. Teaching style

Over the last four decades, we learned that different people absorb information differently depending on how they respond to different information presentation methods. Some individuals learn best from reading texts. Some by watching video lectures. Some by doing worksheets that introduce new information in tiny incremental amounts. Some via teacher questioning using the Socratic Method. Some by analogy. Some by deduction. The point here is that a teacher may be fully competent to teach half a class, but whose methods are confusing and not helpful to the other half of that class.

Joe needs to understand what kinds of instruction work for him, and then find a class, tutor, video, text, worksheet collection, or online course (or a combination of all) that are most appropriate for him.

4. Language Barriers

(162)

A quick Google search ("professor can't speak English") returns more than 2,000 results, most of which are posts about teachers who cannot communicate well enough to help their students, regardless of their expertise, or teaching ability in their native language. (In our example, Joe speaks American English, but the problem could be just as severe if Joe spoke Hindi as his primary language and had not yet mastered English.)

If the problem is the teacher, Joe needs to follow all the same steps as described above. If the language problem is with Joe, then consider taking a year off from school and instead find an immersive and intense English program where he will read, write, speak, and hear English 12 or more hours a day, 6 days a week, for the next year. The knowledge gained in that year may not only help Joe sail through college upon his return, but may help him in his career for the rest of his life.

Accreditation Issues

Inigo: You keep using that word. I do not think it means what you think it means. (From the film, "The Princess Bride.")

(162)

There are different types of accreditation and different reasons you should care about them. Unfortunately, even some very well-known and very reputable universities will misrepresent themselves or at least keep quiet about their deficiencies, and hope you will not notice.

This chapter exposes you to the misrepresentations and may help you to make an informed decision about the colleges and programs that are vying for your time and money.

There are several reasons you should care about the kinds of accreditation claimed by your school, and just as importantly, your major's department. Before we get into those reasons, it is important to define how we will use the word, "accreditation."

Here is the definition as it applies to this book:

Accreditation: A statement by an organization that either a school or a specific program in the school is considered to be "approved" by the accrediting organization. The accrediting organization may or may not be recognized in any way by other schools, the U.S. government, or by other accrediting agencies who are recognized.

A school not able to achieve accredited by a "recognized" accrediting agency may sometimes obtain this recognition from an "unrecognized" agency or may even invent their own accrediting agency.

A small story (The names of the individual involved and his school have been changed. The goal here is to make a point, not persecute a particular college):

An adult studied for years to earn a Bachelor's degree, dividing his coursework between Psychology and Business Management. While he had a successful career in business, he was also interested in creating a future opportunity as a Counselor should he ever tire of his first career. He had very limited financial means. He and his wife took turns attending college part-time, alternating semesters and both always working full-time. In the end, it took sixteen years to earn his bachelor's degree. He was awarded his Bachelor's degree in 1994.

After his first son was born, he decided to pursue a Master's Degree. He received literature from a number of colleges and spoke to their advisors. However, he did not know what questions to ask and what topics the college advisors knew not to bring up.

He considered programs at a number of universities, and selected an established private university that was almost one hundred years old and "fully accredited" by the "Middle States Commission on Higher Education." This is the same organization that accredits hundreds of colleges including:

- State U of N.Y.(SUNY)
- U.S. Naval Academy
- U of Delaware
- U of Maryland
- U of Pennsylvania
- Drexel University
- Rowan University
- Bryn Mawr College
- Columbia University
- Cornell U

Based on the college's history, reputation, and accreditation, he sat down with one of the college's advisors who advised him that the college's Master of Science in Counseling program would be just perfect for him to pursue a career change into counseling. With few exceptions, the program classes met every other weekend for two years and combined Psychology, Counseling, and Human Resource Management courses in one terrific program.

He applied, was accepted, and started the program. Over the next two years, he experienced terrific teachers and learned much. Despite working fifty or more hours per week to pay his bills, he completed the program in two years with a Grade Point Average of 3.76 out of a possible 4.00. He received his Master of Science Diploma. He is exhausted, broke, but oh so proud and happy to have completed this challenge.

He then proceeds to his first job interview and that is where the story turns weird.

"So, Mr. Smith, I see you went to such-and-such university and did very well. I love their basketball team."

"Thank you."

"However, at our firm, we only hire people with accredited Master of Science degrees."

"What do you mean?"

"While your university is fully accredited, their Master of Science in Counseling program is not. In fact, what you took was a 36-credit program. The national organization that accredits those programs changed over the last few years and the standard is now 48 credits for this kind of degree. As a matter of fact, not only do you need 12 more credits, but there may be additional required courses based on newer standards."

In shock, the job applicant asks, "When did these standards change?"

The interviewer replies, "Oh, about four or five years ago."

"So, if I just take the four courses equaling the missing 12 credits, will that be acceptable?"

"No, your degree will still be from an unaccredited program even though the overall school is accredited."

The applicant seethed and went home. He then called several other employers and colleges and confirmed the new information. In fact, he also learned that:

a. The additional courses he needed to take were not available at his college.

b. While other colleges would accept some of his credits, they each required their students to take at least 24 out of the required 48 credits of the program at their school. In other words, while all of the student's course credits were technically transferable, only 24 would count toward an accredited Master's Degree at another college. The rest of the credits would have to be earned by paying for and taking all the other courses over again.

c. The advisor at his college knew darn well that they were selling an unaccredited program, but did not bring up that topic to insure they filled their seats.

What have we learned from this little extremely painful story? (It was certainly painful for the student.)

Lessons Learned:

1. Just because a University or College is accredited, that does not mean your specific program is accredited.

2. Even if you attend a well-known and fully accredited university, other universities may cap the number of credits they will accept for transfer.

3. College recruiters and advisors are there to fill seats even if it means neglecting to disclose that certain aspects of their program may not be in the student's best interest.

There are other accreditation topics that you need to learn. This is truly a case of "buyer beware." Let us start with the reasons one cares about accreditation at all:

Reasons to Care About Course/Program Accreditation	
1	Transferability
2	Employer Acceptance
3	Acceptance for Advanced Degree Admission
4	Public Acceptance
5	Licensure

Transferability

Transferability Story #1

In December of my senior year in high school, I was informally "invited not to return" by my high school's Disciplinary Vice Principal. (Yes, there is a whole story behind that statement, but that story will wait for another book.) In January of what would have been my senior year, I started taking courses at my local community college, (Camden County Community College or CCC). I had outstanding teachers. My grades were also excellent.

In the fall, I transferred to Temple University in Philadelphia. Temple and my community college are both accredited by the same organization. Also, Temple has had positive experiences with the preparedness of transfer students from CCC. As a result, Temple accepted all of my CCC credits as applied toward my eventual 120 that would be required for my Bachelor's degree.

My intention at that time was to remain at Temple and complete my degree there. However, an unexpected job promotion and transfer from Philadelphia, Pennsylvania, to Wilton, Connecticut caused a change of plans.

In the years that followed, I started taking courses at the University of Bridgeport (UB). Due to scheduling issues (I was still working long hours), some of the courses I needed were not available at UB when I was available. However, I was able to take those courses at Fairfield University and Housatonic Community College.

My advisor at UB made sure I was aware of the limited quantity of courses UB would accept toward my Bachelor's degree.

As a result, I limited my outside courses and most were successfully transferred to UB.

Transferability Story #2

Paul (not his real name), one of my older son's best friends had a tough time in high school. So much so, that he did not realize how truly capable and intelligent he was. As a result, he decided to apply to ITT, a college with a reputation for accepting anyone who could pay. Warnings from friends about possible accreditation issues were explained away by the college recruiter.

Paul decided he wanted to study technology. He was impressed with the courses offered at ITT Technical Institute. ITT was large, had campuses nationwide, and the ITT website represented that the school was accredited by the "Accrediting Council for Independent Colleges and Schools." (Sounds impressive, doesn't it?)

Paul comes from a hard-working family that does not have a lot of money. As a result, he scrambled to borrow money from multiple sources so he could get a good education. Between government loans, private loans, and family loans, he borrowed about $50,000 to cover his first two years of college education. (114)

Paul spent two years to earn his Associates Degree (a two-year degree) from ITT. He studied hard and got great grades.

Paul was hired as an electronic drafter by a major engineering firm. He loves his job and even got a raise in his first six months on the job where his salary was increased to just under $30,000 per year.

However, Paul saw that he made less than half the salary of programmers with a bachelor's degree.

With his self-esteem finally built from his great grades and employer appreciation, Paul decided to research his options for a bachelor's degree, despite his $50,000 in outstanding student loans. With an associate's degree, Paul only theoretically needed two more years of college for his Bachelor of Science in technology. After all, a bachelor's degree could conceivably double his income and enable him to pay back his loans. Paul started to contact four-year colleges in our area.

Paul quickly found out that no regionally accredited four-year school he spoke with would accept his ITT credits.

At every school Paul contacted, they dismissed the value of ITT accreditation by the "Accrediting Council for Independent Colleges and Schools."

His bachelor's degree options were:

1. Forget about his ITT associate's degree and start his bachelor's education from scratch. Of course, he cannot "forget" about his $50,000 in ITT college loans.

2. Try to pass one or more courses via credit-by-exam even though he is now months or years removed from taking those courses. A concern with this approach was that the content of some of the courses at ITT were indeed not as rigorous as the content of the accredited programs. There might have to be lengthy self-study prior to taking each one of those exams.

3. Accept the fact that he might need to borrow another $50,000 and return to ITT for his bachelor's degree, as they were the only place that would recognize his associates degree. Of course, this will be of little help should he later wish to apply for jobs at employers who only hire employees who have regionally accredited degrees. (This was before the federal government took steps to shut down ITT.)

4. Give up on the idea of a bachelor's degree, as it will take him 10 to 20 years to pay off the $50,000 in debt he already has from his ITT associate's degree.

Had Paul wanted to keep an option for eventually getting a Bachelor's degree from any of our area's four-year schools, he might have benefitted from doing a little web surfing prior to attending ITT.

Here is how one attorney's web site describes the situation:

> Many for-profit career schools or colleges represent that they are accredited and that credits or degrees from their schools will transfer. Most of them claim to be accredited by The Accrediting Council for Independent Colleges and Schools (ACICS) or they just claim to be accredited without providing the name of the institution accrediting them. However, many public institutions... do not recognize accreditation by the Accrediting Council for Independent Colleges and Schools. (http://www.schoolscamlawyer.com/college-accreditation-fraud/) [40]

Again, ITT is only the most publicly visible of the many questionably accredited schools you should avoid.

Now there are other reasons a course may be rejected for transfer by a college. Some colleges may not allow courses "core" to your major to be transferred. Some colleges may not accept a course if another college has a reputation for grade inflation. Some colleges will not accept transfer of courses more than seven years old. However, one of the most common reasons is that the school itself is not accredited by an agency they respect.

One way some schools avoid addressing the issue is to steer the conversation and make the claim, "We are recognized by the U.S. Department of Education." That statement will be true. It was true of ITT. (It is also true of any number of vocational schools.) Recognition by the U.S. Department of Education in no way determines if the school is worth going to. This should be ignored as an irrelevant statement. In no way does such recognition imply that their accreditation will be accepted by other schools for the purposes of credit transfer.

[Note: After writing the first draft of this book, but prior to publication, the U.S. government finally cracked down on ITT Tech. As of December 10, 2016, the school is finally out of business. However, ITT is not the only school with sub-standard accreditation and educational offerings. The lessons we draw from ITT apply to many other schools as well.]

[Second Note: Charter Oak State College's web site describes a possible program to help ITT students. Here is text as of 2/20/2017 from the web site: [161]

"Let us help you transfer

Are you an ITT Tech student affected by the recent closure? We want to help. For over 40 years Charter Oak State College has been assisting adult learners in completing their degrees and we would like to do the same for you. Charter Oak State College is Connecticut's public online college. We have evaluated three ITT Tech programs of study for credit transfer to Charter Oak's Cyber Security or Business Administration majors.

The ITT Tech programs evaluated for credit are the Associate of Science, Business Management; Bachelor of Applied Science, Information Systems & Cybersecurity; and Bachelor of Science, Information Systems & Cybersecurity.

Course equivalency guides and more information is available for review. The guides will outline the specific courses that we will accept for transfer. Once a student has transferred to Charter Oak, they can complete their degrees conveniently through the exclusive use of Charter Oak's 8 and 15-week courses. Our advising team is looking forward to assisting you!

Students interested in transferring into Charter Oak State College's Cyber Security or Business Administration program can start the process by reviewing the Guides and contacting the College at <u>admissions@charteroak.edu</u>." [161]

Trustworthy Accrediting Organizations

In my experience, there are only seven organizations whose accreditations are accepted by reputable schools. Those organizations are:

The "Big Seven" Accrediting Organizations:

- Middle States Commission on Higher Education, formerly part of the Middle States Association of Colleges and Schools.

- New England Association of Schools and Colleges.

- Higher Learning Commission.

- Northwest Accreditation Commission and Northwest Commission on Colleges and Universities (NWCCU).

- Southern Association of Colleges and Schools.

- Western Association of Schools and Colleges.

- Accrediting Commission for Community and Junior Colleges,

- Source: Wikipedia: https://en.wikipedia.org/wiki/Regional_accreditation 4/20/2016

(131)

Even so, if you are certain you will need to transfer your credit from one school to another, contact the destination school, and ask some questions.

Also, remember how the accreditation of certain universities may be acceptable, but that their individual programs may not.

Another small story: Fred and Ned

Fred and Ned (not their real names) went to a recruitment session at a major state college that bragged about how many of their students later went to the state's most well-known graduate school. Fred and Ned applied, were accepted, and then attended that major state school. Fred majored in Electrical Engineering. Ned majored in Physics. Both Fred and Ned earned excellent grades and a Bachelor's degree. Both applied to that graduate school. The graduate school accepted Fred but not Ned. According to the graduate school, Fred's major was sufficiently accredited but Ned's major was not.

The lesson here: Don't accept a statement like "Many of our students went on to study at such-and-such graduate school." If you want that to be an option, call the graduate school and ask if your desired undergraduate program of study will be acceptable to them. This is your life and even some otherwise great colleges will have administrators, teachers, and recruiters whose words must be validated by you, the customer.

Employer Acceptance

In the last story, I managed to slam ITT Tech pretty hard. Here is another aspect of that story. My son's friend Paul did ultimately leverage his Associate's Degree at ITT into an entry-level technical job that he enjoyed. Yes, the pay was less than at many similar technical jobs offered by other employers. However, it did give him a start to his career.

In the same month that ITT was shut down, Paul was terminated from his job. The reason given by the employer was that while Paul knew the basics, that he was "insufficiently trained" when compared to other electronic drafts-persons. As I write this, Paul is depressed and his college debt does not correlate with the value of his marketable skills.

There are just over 2,400 4-year colleges in the U.S. and just over 1,600 2-year colleges. [5] While some employers like Google or Facebook can demand applicants come from what they consider the top one percent of colleges, the fact is that there are a wide spectrum of employers and a correspondingly wide spectrum of their expectations.

Some employers do not care and will not check to see if an applicant is from a school accredited by the "Big Seven" organizations. Some care deeply and filter out applicants from schools not accredited by those organizations.

If the purpose of a STEM education is to provide you with the widest possible range of employment opportunities and compensation, checking out how employers view your credential is possible but not easy.

Let us go back to the claims by individual schools. Within an online marketing video posted by ITT Tech on YouTube.com (https://www.youtube.com/watch?v=LRFgNJQsSqQ), ITT Tech stated, "More than 14,000 organizations hired ITT Technical Institute graduates in 2011-12. We invited employers across the United States -- from Boeing to Universal Studios -- to talk about the relationship they have with ITT Technical Institute, and to share observations about the ITT Tech graduates they have hired."

Therefore, ITT is HUGE and their graduates went to work SOMEWHERE. Were they paid what graduates from four-year schools accredited by one of the "Big Seven" made? If I run across an authoritative comparison, I will post it on www.thestemstudentsurvivalguide.com/feedback.

When it comes to STEM professions in general, specific program accreditations may be the most important. For examples of specialized accreditations from law to medicine to engineering to social work, check out this web page from the University of Pennsylvania at http://www.collegefactual.com/colleges/university-of-pennsylvania/academic-life/accreditation/. [112]

Acceptance for Advanced Degree Basis

All of the warnings I gave you about being concerned about your degree being acceptable at another college should you decide to pursue a graduate degree or a doctorate also apply.

Public Acceptance

There are times when accreditation is just not important. For much of my childhood and young adult life, my favorite talk radio personality was Dr. Bernard Meltzer. His wide-ranging advice programs ranged as he announced, "from affairs of the pocketbook to affairs of the heart."

Dr. Meltzer was a city planner by training, with a civil engineering degree from City College of New York (accredited by one of the big seven). He earned his master's degree from the Wharton School at the University of Pennsylvania (also accredited by one of the Big Seven).

However, his rationale for people to address him as "Doctor" was found in his doctoral diploma. As reported in the New York Times in his obituary on March 27, 1998,

"Remember," [the radio announcer intoned at the beginning of each show,] "Dr. Meltzer is not an attorney.'' Come to think of it, his doctorate -- a mail-in degree in philosophy, economics, and finance from the unaccredited Columbia Pacific University in California -- was not all that kosher, either." [158]

In the days before the invention of Google, people called him Dr. Meltzer and no one cared where he got his doctorate.

Before you jump at the shortcut of buying a degree from what are derisively called, "Degree Mills," know that other people have had much different experiences with their "fake" doctorates. Google news searches reveal many people who were terminated from their jobs when their educational credentials turned out to be either unaccredited or what I sometimes call "insufficiently accredited."

If you need a whack on the side of the head in order to instill enough fear to keep you away from truly phony schools, any of John Bear's books on degree mills (such as at http://www.amazon.com/Degree-Mills-Billion-Dollar-Industry-Diplomas/dp/1616145072) should do the trick.

Licensure

After graduation, will you want the ability to sit for a professional state or national licensing exam in Nursing, Medicine, Law, Engineering, or any of more than one hundred other professions? If so, be sure to find out if your college is suitably accredited by whatever organization will be testing you. No sense in studying for four years only to be told to start over elsewhere!

The previously noted web page at the University of Pennsylvania should give you an idea of who you need to research for your particular future STEM profession.

The number of "fully accredited" colleges and universities who offer programs that are NOT accredited by their respective professional licensing authorities is truly awe inspiring.

Just a thought…

I struggled with how to characterize what I consider to be "legitimate" accreditation in this book. With regard to each overall school, I guess I could have used the term "Big Seven Accreditation" or "Regional Accreditation" or "Non-scam accreditation."

Then there are the specific bodies that accredit programs in Nursing, Biology, Chemistry, each Engineering specialty, etc.

Your best starting point is the University of Pennsylvania page that lists the bodies that accredit their programs at: http://www.collegefactual.com/colleges/university-of-pennsylvania/academic-life/accreditation/# [112]

If a college you are considering has a major whose program is accredited by some organization not on the U of P web page, your "Spidey Sense" should be tingling with a tiny bit of alarm and motivate you to do a little online research of your own!

What About Hands-On Learning?

I remember being impressed on a tour of Lafayette College when the student leading the tour explained that Lafayette engineering students were given welding instruction their first week of school and then were given the opportunity to spend from five to fifteen hours per week in the various labs for their entire four years of STEM education.

At Lafayette, we toured lab after lab where undergraduate students were conducting all kinds of experiments and/or construction as they slowly but surely mastered the real-life tools of their trade.

Our guide explained that the lab time enabled students to see how the theoretical concepts taught in class could actually be applied in real life. For some, the lab time made the homework tolerable and kept morale high.

I also remember being initially amazed when the engineering student guiding our tour at Rutgers showed us the tens of millions of dollars of lab buildings and equipment on the tour of that college. When I asked a couple of probing questions, my amazement turned to disgust when he disclosed that most of that equipment was off-limits to undergrads and typically used only by professors doing research and their graduate students.

To show those facilities without making the disclosures that came out in our conversation strikes me as bordering on fraudulent. (On the positive side, both Rutgers homecoming and school spirit are "**awesome**.")

In the spirit of full disclosure, as of this writing, I have confirmation from three Rowan students (one majoring Biomedical Engineering, one in Chemical Engineering, and one in Electrical Engineering,) that they have been intensively using Rowan's labs and engineering facilities since their first semester at that college.

One reason I contrast Rowan and Rutgers is that they are both fully accredited New Jersey state universities that charge similar tuition and offer similar programs. When some politicians advocated transferring affiliation and operation of Rutgers' satellite campus in Camden, New Jersey, many Camden Rutgers professors protested, citing Rutgers superior national reputation. Based on the questionable quality of STEM education offered at Rutgers, I would be very cautious accepting a Rutgers education if I was also accepted by Rowan.

I also remember touring a state college that did not officially have STEM accredited programs, but which offered two years of classroom only instruction (i.e. minimal lab facilities, if at all,) after which students could transfer to their "partner" school, which was a highly accredited engineering school in another part of the state. When my son and I later toured the partner school, I was surprised to learn that each year, the partner school only accepted a tiny percentage of those students who applied from the feeder school. ("We only have so much room for transfers," the dean explained.) This impressed me as another case bordering on fraud.

The hands-on aspect provided by some colleges should be mimicked by others. Access to these kinds of facilities outside of the typical 1 to 3 hours per week required by certain courses such as Chemistry, differentiate some colleges from others. That access may be reflected in lower failure rates. If so, the additional cost for those colleges may be well worth it.

There are also courses where a certain number of supervised internship or practice hours in a professional environment are required. I have more to say about them later in the text.

Personal Choices and Value Balancing

Peer Pressure to Balance Work and Play

Part of the "college experience," is learning how to balance work and play without Mommy and Daddy looking over your shoulder. Due mainly to financial constraints, my wife and I attended college part-time and over many years while working full time. While others have praised our dedication and while it is true that we were often able to bring our work experience directly into the classroom, many of my friends not only had more fun in their early twenties, but their careers progressed much faster as employers often promote only after degrees are earned.

It is for these considerations, that I encourage people to go to college full time if their finances permit.

Much of the learning when it comes to balancing work and play is something not addressed in any of the forty courses you will take in a STEM program, yet it's one of the most important lessons to be learned.

When it comes to how people learn, the famed Psychologist Alfred Bandura originated the concept of "Social Learning Theory" which explains that humans generally learn by observing others. In most college environments, this reality can be deadly to the success of a STEM student.

In most college dormitories and apartments, students with a variety of majors live, play, and study in close quarters with each other.

Annual national surveys of college students showed that those majoring in business and the social sciences generally study closer to about 14 hours a week than any other number of hours. Meanwhile, engineering students reported not only that they typically studied about 19 hours a week, but also that they often arrived at class without completing a higher percentage of their homework than their non-STEM peers. [113] [114] Considering that 40% to 60% of STEM students fail out, it is not unreasonable to assume that those who study the "typical" 19 hours per week have about that chance of failing out.

Rationally and intellectually, the STEM students know that they have chosen a tough four years of college so they may have a rewarding forty years of work after college. The fact that studying an extra hour per day results in STEM failure rates of 40% to 60% does not communicate to the subconscious that 30 to 40 hours of homework might what is required for STEM students taking five courses per semester.

After all, those STEM students see themselves studying long after their peers have stopped for a swim, run, or game of Beer Pong. How much can a person take?

Some schools have tried to address this situation by segregating student housing by major. This is a small step toward dealing with the issue. But only a small step.

Little Story #1 - Rose

The following story has been told to me in various flavors by different family members. Here are the pieces common to all versions:
I have a niece named Rose (not her real name). Rose is the youngest of three children. When she was young, she observed how both of her older siblings seemed to struggle through high school. When Rose graduated from Middle School, she gathered three of her girlfriends. She explained to her friends that they should form a study group that would meet every day after school at Rose's house if they could not complete their work at school. They agreed that the girls who finished early would help those still working.

The girls kept their commitment to each other. They took tough courses and supported each other. Rose's mother made sure there were always snacks available. Rose still enjoyed other aspects of high school. She was an athlete and a cheerleader, and a musician. However, school and the study group came first. The four girls graduated with stellar rankings in their high school and all graduated from college.

Little Story #2 - Jerry

Jerry is my youngest son. In high school, he was a very busy young man. He was an active member of a very busy high school youth group. He competitively swam year-round on both High School and Club swim teams. He practiced swimming ten hours a week and spent almost as much time working out in the gym. He scored in the top quarter of people who took the SATs his junior year. He was the co-captain of the High School Swim Team. His grades were pretty good, (but not in the top decile of those in his class). He was very active socially and attended religious school right through the end of high school. By his senior year, Jerry has more than a 1,000 Facebook "friends." By "friends," I mean people who knew Jerry outside of the virtual world.

At our swim club, at our synagogue, and in our neighborhood, I was no longer Leon. Now, I was "Jerry's Dad."

As Jerry toured various colleges, he paid attention to the answers given by college administrators as I grilled them about failure rates at the end of their presentations. He was also painfully aware of how his older brother had struggled when he majored in engineering in college.

Jerry, who decided to attend Rowan University, also had many friends who decided to attend Rowan. A number of them approached Jerry and asked to room with him. As much as he valued his friendships, Jerry knew he needed some help if he would not be a member of the portion of the STEM student body that became miserable in college. The college sponsored some pre-college activities to help freshman meet new people.

Jerry gently grilled each person he met. "What is your major? What was your rank in high school? How committed are you to doing well in college?" Jerry considered their responses and then selected three others who he recruited as his freshman roommates. All three graduated at the top of their classes in high school and all three were STEM majors. "Look," Jerry would explain, "girls, partying, and athletics might all be fun, but I'm here to get good grades and succeed. If you are here to make school a higher priority than all the other stuff, then room with me. I'm willing to do what it takes here because I would like to make a boatload of money after graduating."

Jerry and his roommates struggled, but succeeded. About half of the freshman engineering students disappeared from Jerry's classes by the end of the year. It was not easy, but Jerry and his roommates did not fail out.

In both of these stories of success, Rose and Jerry succeeded in part because they isolated themselves from people who were not going to model the homework and studying behavior they needed to adopt.

If you are a STEM student who is surrounded by non-STEM students, you already have a psychological strike against you before you even begin.

However, for many, those who live at home and either commute to school or attend only online, the odds are even worse. Without a social support system, the odds of finding reasons to fail may be even greater. While my wife and I succeeded as a group of two, the thousands of commuting failures do not make for pretty reporting.

Meditation

This is another topic where one would think that colleges would educate incoming students. (Yet one would again be wrong.)

Over the last fifty years, there has been a large volume amount of research done on the relationship of meditation to academic performance. The results of earlier studies were mixed with some showing substantial benefits and some showing none at all.

Just as no medicine works for every patient, meditation is not for everyone. HOWEVER, in a recent study, students who were self-identified as having problems focusing performed better on quizzes if they learned how to meditate for less than ten minutes a day. [7]

If you are such a person, it is time to do a little Googling and learn about this topic.

Sports... Maybe... Maybe Not

There are many studies correlating physical activity with academic success. [8] During Jerry's time in high school, I used to share my amazement with other parents of competitive swimmers, that these kids did great academically despite spending two or more hours a day in the pool and another hour a day in the gym. The repeated consensus was that as swimmers learned to value every hundredth of a second in performance, they learned to focus their attention in the classroom and focus on time management when it came to homework.

At the college level, successful STEM students who participated in high school elite sports often choose a different path. My son, Jerry decided against trying out for his college's swim team and instead opted for the less time-consuming "club" swim team to free as much time as possible for home homework.

If you are not the athletic type, do not dwell on the subject. My wife, someone who never participated in any organized sport, attended college while working long hours in full time jobs. In only one undergrad course and only one graduate level course did she ever earn a "B" instead of an "A."

As for me, I have a genetic disorder that causes (among other things) very painful joints. This kept me in bed or on crutches for most of seventh and eighth grades. I attended a three-story high school where unable to walk stairs, I was fortunate to have a key to the only elevator. In college, my own undergraduate

Grade Point Average was 3.67 and my graduate school GPA was 3.76 (each out of 4.00).

While physical activity may help grades for some, the examples set by my wife and I show it is not absolutely necessary.

Consider the report of time devoted to athletics as reported by Student Athletes:

Total Sport Hours/Day In-Season (Weekday)						
Division I						
	Baseball	Men's Basketball	Football	All other Men's Sports	Women's Basketball	All Other Women's Sports
Average Time in Hours	5.9	5.6	6.4	5.2	5.6	6.0
% Reporting Sport 6+ Hours/Day	48%	38%	52%	32%	32%	29%

(148)

The bottom line here is every athlete's personal struggle to balance the hours per day required to pass STEM courses [114] with the time demands for practice and play placed on many college athletes. [148]

Drugs – The Good Kind

My oldest son had attention and self-control problems in grades one, two, and three. Suspicious of how society often turns too quickly to medications, my wife and I sought out occupational therapists, play therapists, a "natural" oriented physician, and other approaches as well. Considering my own degrees in Psychology and Counseling, my bookshelf quickly filled with texts on how to treat the "problem child."

My son was increasingly unhappy in school, (even after we changed schools) and increasingly became disruptive.

After three years and many efforts, my wife and I felt like failures as we sat down with a pediatric psychiatrist who understood our concerns and positions.

After a review of all of our efforts and two interviews with our son, she suggested we consider Ritalin, a drug very chemically similar to caffeine in safety, mechanism of action, risks, and side effects.

Similar to caffeine? I wanted to know how a stimulant would enable my son to focus and behave calmly. On the surface, this did not make sense.

The doctor explained that the working theory behind people with self-control and attention problems is that there is a hormone manufactured in the brain that enables us to have self-control. Stimulant drugs like caffeine and Ritalin are thought to stimulate the brain to make more of the hormones related to self-control.

In my son's case, the Ritalin was immediately effective and the side effects minimal. His behavior changed for the better. His grades improved and stayed improved through the rest of elementary school, through middle school, and through high school.

That does not mean that Ritalin or other medications are for everyone. There are side effects about which you should talk over with your doctor.

In my own case, the discovery of caffeine as a young adult was certainly one of the factors that enabled me to do well at work and in school. (Diet soda started my day in my twenties and thirties and multiple cups of coffee ever since.)

There are other attention deficit and self-control medications in addition to the ones discussed here. If you have an issue, go to a doctor and deal with it before you need years of therapy to deal with the psychological damage to your self-esteem because you failed out of college.

Side note: Another parent in my community had a daughter in high school who was prescribed Ritalin. When her doctor suggested that self-control and focusing problems sometimes run in families, he visited his own family doctor. He shared with me that starting Ritalin at age 50 enabled him to make dramatically better business decisions.

The Centers for Disease Control (at CDC.gov) provides easy to understand descriptions and layperson tools for identifying Attention Deficit/Hyperactivity Disorder (ADHD). [149]

The following page contains an excerpt from their website.

People with ADHD show a persistent pattern of inattention and/or hyperactivity-impulsivity that interferes with functioning or development:

1. **Inattention: Six or more symptoms of inattention for children up to age 16, or five or more for adolescents 17 and older and adults; symptoms of inattention have been present for at least 6 months, and they are inappropriate for developmental level:**
   - o   Often fails to give close attention to details or makes careless mistakes in schoolwork, at work, or with other activities.
   - o   Often has trouble holding attention on tasks or play activities.
   - o   Often does not seem to listen when spoken to directly.
   - o   Often does not follow through on instructions and fails to finish schoolwork, chores, or duties in the workplace (e.g., loses focus, side-tracked).
   - o   Often has trouble organizing tasks and activities.
   - o   Often avoids, dislikes, or is reluctant to do tasks that require

---

mental effort over a long period of time (such as schoolwork or homework).
- ○ Often loses things necessary for tasks and activities (e.g. school materials, pencils, books, tools, wallets, keys, paperwork, eyeglasses, mobile telephones).
- ○ Is often easily distracted
- ○ Is often forgetful in daily activities.

2. **Hyperactivity and Impulsivity: Six or more symptoms of hyperactivity-impulsivity for children up to age 16, or five or more for adolescents 17 and older and adults; symptoms of hyperactivity-impulsivity have been present for at least 6 months to an extent that is disruptive and inappropriate for the person's developmental level:**
- ○ Often fidgets with or taps hands or feet, or squirms in seat.
- ○ Often leaves seat in situations when remaining seated is expected.
- ○ Often runs about or climbs in situations where it is not appropriate (adolescents or adults may be limited to feeling restless).
- ○ Often unable to play or take part in leisure activities quietly.
- ○ Is often "on the go" acting as if "driven by a motor".
- ○ Often talks excessively.
- ○ Often blurts out an answer before a question has been completed.
- ○ Often has trouble waiting his/her turn.
- ○ Often interrupts or intrudes on others (e.g., butts into conversations or games)

In addition, the following conditions must be met:

- • Several inattentive or hyperactive-impulsive symptoms were present before age 12 years.
- • Several symptoms are present in two or more setting, (such as at home, school or work; with friends or relatives; in other activities).
- • There is clear evidence that the symptoms interfere with, or reduce the quality of, social, school, or work functioning.
- • The symptoms are not better explained by another mental disorder (such as a mood disorder, anxiety disorder, dissociative disorder, or a personality disorder). The symptoms do not happen only during the course of schizophrenia or another psychotic

disorder.

Based on the types of symptoms, three kinds (presentations) of ADHD can occur:

Combined Presentation: if enough symptoms of both criteria inattention and hyperactivity-impulsivity were present for the past 6 months

Predominantly Inattentive Presentation: if enough symptoms of inattention, but not hyperactivity-impulsivity, were present for the past six months

Predominantly Hyperactive-Impulsive Presentation: if enough symptoms of hyperactivity-impulsivity but not inattention were present for the past six months.

Because symptoms can change over time, the presentation may change over time as well. (149)

ADHD in Adults

ADHD often lasts into adulthood. For more information about diagnosis and treatment throughout the lifespan, please visit the websites of the National Resource Center on ADHD and the National Institutes of Mental Health. (149)

More About Life Balance
All work and no play.... makes Jack a psychopathic maniac

Sam (not his real name) was one of my best friends as a teen and young adult. His first year as an engineering student at Drexel was a washout. Sam really did spend too little time on homework and too much time partying.

Mike (also not his real name), his roommate, was a more studious type. When Mike was not in class, he was in the room, at his desk, studying. Mike was still connected with his girlfriend in high school, and she lived hundreds of miles away from school. This was from a pre-internet and pre-cellphone era and so they had no connection during the semester. (In those days, telephone calls beyond the local county were considered "long distance" and too costly for regular communications by impoverished college students.)

In high school, Mike had appeared to be a well-adjusted person, earning good grades, participating in extra-curricular activities, and had a half-dozen good friends.

In college, Mike kept to himself. He attended no parties and made no college friends. He did not drink or touch marijuana. In hindsight, it must have been painfully lonely. Mike spent all of his waking hours seriously focused on his studies.

One night, Mike decided that his existence was both painful and pointless. He stripped naked and repeatedly ran up and down the hallway shrieking at the top of his lungs. Medics and the police were called. Mike was strapped down to a gurney and taken away. No one in the dorm ever heard from Mike again.

The next year, Sam transferred to another college and started his studies from scratch. He still had fun, but balanced the partying with more study time. Sam graduated near the bottom of his class and attended college a total of five years, including his washout year at Drexel, but he still graduated. He went on to have a successful career as a nuclear engineer.

The moral of the story? Just as you need the time to study, sleep, and exercise, as a primate, you also need to maintain connections with other human beings.

If an "elite" athletic team is too much of a time commitment, consider a "club" team. If one fraternity makes too many demands in terms of social activities, choose another. Even if you do not believe in God, a college social group representing your family's religion may keep you well-adjusted and able to deal with the stresses of college.

A common bastardization of Ecclesiastes 9:11 goes like this:

"The race does not always go to the swiftest, nor the battle to the strongest, nor bread to the wise, nor riches to men of understanding. . . but that is sure as heck the way to bet."

"Muscle through" five Weeder courses a semester by eliminating all non-academic interactions? Sure, you can try. However, the odds are against you. Would you want to go to a doctor or employ an engineer who did not have the common sense to pursue solutions with the highest chance of success?

Sleep to Remember

(162)

You would think that it is in your college's best interest to prepare you for college. (Or at least validate that your high school did so.) Many colleges are research institutions. However, with regard to communicating the research on how to succeed in college, most do a terrible job.

In my previous chapter dealing with homework, I noted how Psychologist Alfred Bandura's "Social Learning Theory" explains how the behavior modeled by others powerfully influences our own behavior. When it comes to bad college habits modeled by one's peers, sleep is a topic worthy of discussion.

We have learned much in the last decade about how we think the brain operates. During the day, your experiences are recorded in an area of the brain devoted to short-term memory. At night, during the deepest part of sleep known as REM, those memories are transferred to the various parts of the brain where long-term memories are imprinted. With limited, interrupted, or poor sleep, your brain may store some or none of that information and some or all of the previous day will be forgotten.

Let us try to put this in perspective.

You decide to pursue a STEM career for any or all of the reasons covered in the beginning of the book. You understand the high failure rates among very intelligent STEM students. You understand that most STEM courses are taught in ten-week increments, with most having three classes per week. You also understand that in many STEM topics, information learned one day might serve as the foundation to understand the next. Losing one day of information can trigger a snowball effect of confusion that can lead to failure or at least a low grade for an entire course.

One weeknight binging on Netflix results in limited sleep can cause you to lose not just a day of learning, but can be the tipping point that leads to a bad semester.

"But this is college," you say. Smoking dope, screwing until dawn, binging on Netflix, and playing video games for ten-hour marathons are all part of the college experience.

"Yes," I reply. "But you need to make a decision. Are you ready to jeopardize a three-to-four-million-dollar career because focusing on school for four years is just too hard? The choice is yours."

If you are going to do any or all of the naughty things, why not actually plan for them? If you have Friday classes, do not go out Friday night. Instead, go to bed early Friday, allow your brain to integrate those long-term memories, and then plan for a wild Saturday night.

Yes, some non-STEM kids will be partying from Friday at sundown until Monday at dawn. Some of them are destined for whole careers of low-paying misery. Are you?

What about the ability to focus during the day in order to store those short-term memories for nighttime transfer to long-term storage?

We have known for a long time that Alzheimer patients suffer from a build-up of excessive deposits of beta-amyloid proteins in the brain. The buildups are associated with the gradual death of brain cells. Again, recent studies give us clues and theories based on evidence.

Your brain is bathed in Cerebro-spinal Fluid. At the beginning of your day, the fluid is generally clear of beta-amyloid proteins. One theory is that during the normal brain operation during the day, beta-amyloid proteins appear in the brain as a byproduct of normal brain operation. Think of it as brain poop. Your body's normal and healthy digestive processes produce brain poop.

We know from the Alzheimer's studies, that normal, restful sleep, is when the body naturally washes out the beta-amyloid proteins that were generated during the day. We know that repeated instances of poor sleep causes accumulations of these toxic proteins, which damage brain cells and interfere with not just with memory storage, but also with brain functioning in general. Just as constipation will first make you miserable, and may eventually lead to a perforated bowel and nasty, even fatal infections, so too will lack of sleep first reduce your ability to learn, and eventually damage your brain.

So not only is good sleep required to store memories of the day that just happened, but that good sleep in the days and weeks prior to today are what is required for your brain to function clearly during that expensive day of school. (There are no inexpensive school days.)

Once again, your school will probably house you with student from all kinds of majors. Just as many of these majors require less than half of the homework of many STEM majors, so too will many of those majors require less focus, learning, and attention in the classroom.

The United States Army understands the functioning of a well-rested soldier depends in part on the soldier's long-term sleep experiences. Housing new troops together in barracks and enforcing a communal "lights out" is not only healthy, but causes people to be exposed to healthy behavior modeled by others.

Your college dorm will never be an Army barracks. You need to be aware of the powerful influence the modeled behavior of others will have on your own subconscious and your own behavioral urges.

If he was real, Master Yoda might say, "Your destiny, your peers do not have to be. Self-aware, you must become."

Training Her Brain [162]

Learning and Retaining

For the majority of STEM students, the transition from high school to college brings a shock when they realize that the workload is so much more burdensome than high school, and that their old approaches no longer work. Cram the night before an exam? Do a four-week paper the weekend before it is due? Despite coming from an environment of good grades and SAT scores, the washout rates are enormous.

We've already covered what you can do about your learning ENVIRONMENT. Now we will address the learning process itself.

Get to class. Get to class early. Sit where you will not be distracted by side conversations or people to whom you are physically attracted.

Bring your laptop computer and be sure it is fully charged and had plenty of disk space. In your backpack, be sure to bring your charging cable and an external battery just in case you are mistaken. There are no do-overs. You are serious about this class.

When the teacher talks, pay attention and take your notes electronically IF APPROPRIATE.

Your teacher is a human being with all the frailties of human beings. Their teaching style may or may not match your learning style. Tough. This is your battle to win and no excuse will be accepted.

Don't write down every syllable the teacher utters. Your mission is to note those points that are likely to either be the foundation for later topics or are likely to be the subject of tests and quizzes.

Most teachers welcome questions. Some do not. If you have a question that has not been sufficiently answered, be a pest. You don't care if other students want to get out of class early. You want your four-million-dollar career. Screw them if they are in a rush.

Record your questions in your notes.

Some teachers permit recording of the class. Teachers who are either insecure or incompetent will not. In any case, if you are taking good notes, recording of the class may become your lame excuse not to pay close attention to what is being said.

On the first day of class, figure out whether the teacher has college-level communication skills. If you cannot clearly understand them to the point where you will understand complex explanations, walk out, go to your advisor, and do not back down your demand to withdraw from the course. Even if it costs you an extra semester or even an extra year of college, the misery of a teacher who cannot communicate is never worth "just trying."

If the teacher speaks clear English, but you determine during the first week that their teaching style is not going to work for you, walk out, go to your advisor, and do not back down your demand to withdraw from the course. You are a paying customer. If you pay thousands of dollars for an inferior service, you will have no one to blame but yourself. Either this is the person who will be your partner in passing the course or the teacher is part of the system that you need to be wary of.

In the distant future, the problems with teachers who do not deliver the student's money's worth may be resolved. But probably not during your college career.

•

What Many Fail to Learn in High School

Including Lecture Hall classes, a teacher may have hundreds of students per year. Many of the students will considered by the teacher to either be non-entities or annoyances.

For many students, references from their teachers will be the first references presented to their first post-college employers.

Also, when in trouble, students are more likely to receive help from a teacher they have favorably impressed.

To learn as much as possible while making a favorable impression, consider the following practices:

- Sit up front
- Sit in the same seat every class period.
- Say your name when you first ask a question and then until the teacher addresses you by your name.
- Show interest.
- Do not use your phone during class.
- Do not even glance at your phone in class.
- No texting, no buzzing.
- Be prepared.
- Never ask a question if the answer can be found in the syllabus.
- Do not ask if the required reading is required.

Internships

(162)

The first batch of college interns I ever hired were fourteen students from Drexel University in 1981. At that time, I was working as an Industrial Engineer at Wheaton Glass Company in Millville, New Jersey. That was thirty-five years ago. Since then, I have hired and/or worked with hundreds of interns representing about a dozen different STEM professions.

In my experience, businesses don't hire interns because they want to support college education, even though they are in favor of such a concept. I have not seen businesses hire interns primarily to see who would make a good permanent hire, even though permanent hiring decisions are often made to those interns whose combination of personal and technical skills make them a great match for that company.

In fact, most companies I have worked for or consulted to, have one over-riding reason to hire interns. That reason is CHEAP LABOR.

Whether we needed some entry level quality assurance performed, writing code that the senior programmers could then tweak, becoming program testers to find bugs, or help the support staff as we rolled out new computers, interns were seen as a source of cheap, temporary labor.

Today, there are all kinds of official laws that say what interns can and cannot do. With STEM interns, my experience has been always to pay above minimum wage, and sometimes two to four times minimum wage, depending on the skills and experience of the intern.

Regardless of why the employer wants to hire you, there are only a few reasons a STEM student should consider an internship:

The Best Internship Reasons

1. To see if the real world is attractive.
2. Because the school requires it.
3. To gain employable skills not taught at school.
4. Because the money prevents dropping out of college.

Let's take a look at each of these reasons:

Positive Reason One: Real World Experience

Twins Nan and Bert (fictional characters in this story) did well in high school chemistry. One of the careers open to people like them and that they were attracted to is that of a pharmacist. After doing a little online research, they were impressed that the median annual income for pharmacists in the United States is $121,871 with good benefits in terms of time off and health insurance. [1]

Pharmacists are literally lifesavers. They are the often the only line of defense when a patient obtains prescriptions from different doctors where interactions could be fatal to the patient. Even their mundane daily tasks of accurately filling prescriptions enable patients to trust that their medications are what their doctors prescribed.

There are stories where patients could not afford their medications and just stopped purchasing them, eventually leading to life threatening situations. It is often the pharmacist they will confide in and often the pharmacist who will consult with their physician to find a less expensive alternative.

According to annual polls conducted by the Gallup organization spanning more than twenty professions visible to the public, only nurses are more respected in terms of their honesty and ethics than pharmacists. [2]

Nan and Bert read some news articles and blogs on the web about the practice of pharmacists. They read with the full understanding that it is the most dissatisfied people who vent and that those people who are not angry about something typically enjoy their lives quietly. Their father often impressed upon them that almost every job has both enjoyable and aggravating aspects and that something that might be perceived as a minor annoyance to one person, might be seen as a disheartening, depressing, and ultimately life destroying experience by someone else.

Ultimately, they applied to and were accepted by a college of pharmacy and both did well in their courses. Like many STEM professions, their college required all pharmacy students to start work in pharmacies part or full time in their first year of school and continue such work during their education.

They started work in a local pharmacy where they were trained to work behind the pharmacy counter and could observe the work the pharmacists really performed.

One of the observations the twins made was how intensely busy their pharmacists were all shift long. They were constantly on the phone with insurance companies and doctors. The insurance companies had a seemingly never-ending series of obstacles to approving certain prescriptions, while some of the doctors and a small number of patients just seemed arrogant or rude.

The job included standing practically the whole shift. One of the pharmacists whined repeatedly about having to work on the day of her child's Saturday baseball games.

Nan felt energized by the pace and intensity of the pharmacist's job. Bert felt anxious and depressed at the thought of rarely having a moment to reflect or sit during the shift and often having to work nights or weekends.

Bert visited his counselor at school. Fortunately, the retail pharmacist is only one of several career paths available to him. Pharmacists work in manufacturing, regulatory enforcement, teaching, marketing, research, and in hospitals. [3] Working in each area includes different kinds of compensation and work environments.

Better that Bert found this out as a freshman than after years of misery. Bert quickly investigated part time work in other areas to find out where he would be happy spending most of his waking adult hours and where he would be miserable. (Nan was perfectly happy with her career at the local pharmacy.)

Positive Reason Two: The school requires it

This one is a no brainer. But consider the other points when choosing what internship to accept.

Positive Reason Three: To gain employable skills

The most in-demand technology jobs have titles like Database Administrator, Software Engineer, Web Developer, Software Developer, Software Architect, and Technical Lead. [4] The common technology majors have titles like Computer Science, Computer Technology, and Computer Programming.

The vast majority of technology jobs in business that I have experienced involve some degree of programming (especially if you include in the definition of programming the various scripting languages built into many types of commercial software products).

The library of assets in use in a given company may include a dozen or more different programming languages, some obscure, and some, like COBOL, Fortran, or Business BASIC, that have not been taught in many colleges for decades.

There will always be some graduates who will be in a position to turn down jobs that require learning of what they consider to be less than leading edge technologies and languages.

But for the rest of us, the willingness to continually learn, and that includes learning "old stuff" is part of what makes us worth six figure incomes to our employers.

In addition, many companies have embraced procedures and technologies that help them manage software development and maintenance using even the newest computer technologies that are too expensive or too specialized to be taught at the college level.

The right internships help students absorb knowledge that will give them a competitive edge over their peers when it comes to getting the jobs they want after college.

Positive Reason Four: You need the money to survive

My wife and I did not borrow money to go to college. If loans were even available in the 1970s, we were not aware of them. In addition, our parents did not consider themselves to be in a position to fund our educations at that time. As a result, we worked full time in positions open to people with high school educations and saved our money. We often took one course or two courses at a time, and then only if the money was available that semester. Occasionally, an employer would pay for part of a course.

As a result, we earned our bachelor degrees after seventeen years of mostly part-time education and only then did we start work on our graduate degrees.

There is a school of thought that our classroom experiences were enhanced by the real-world knowledge we brought into class discussions. There is much truth to that statement. There is also the notion that as we painfully kept our standard of living low enough to afford those classes, we truly appreciated their cost and worked out butts off both to get good grades and passionately learn what we were presented. That is also true.

But from society's perspective, this was a terrible path. In all likelihood, the great salaries we have enjoyed since graduating would have started more than a decade earlier. The greater taxes we would have paid would have benefitted our government's desire to balance the desires to minimize taxes while maximizing social programs. We waited more than a decade to have children and if we started earlier, we may even have had more. After all, society needs more educated kids to take care of older people and to pay for social security.

None of this justifies today's kids from incurring $100,000 of debt for a liberal arts degree that qualifies them to work at Starbucks or McDonalds.

But the earlier you finish your education and start a high paying career, the greater the benefits to both you and society. If you are majoring in a STEM profession that offers a six-figure income and need the internship salary to complete your degree in four to six years, then by all means please do so.

The Worst Internship Reasons

Negative Reason One: Prestige

You have a choice between taking one of two intern jobs. Both companies are in the industry where you want to work. The first pays $10 an hour at a small startup where you will sit in on customer meetings, participate in software design issues, write small pieces of the code, and participate in the testing of a new product. The second job is for one of the top three companies in the industry. You will be paid $25 an hour, and your day divided between scanning online customer complaints for full-time employees to respond to and fetching coffee where you can quietly observe how the major players do their work.

Your future employers are likely to be STEM graduates themselves. (In other words, they will not be dummies.) In all likelihood, they could care less that you interned at the Mayo Clinic, at Apple, at Boeing, or wherever. What they will care about is what you SKILLS YOU ACQUIRED as an intern that can BENEFIT them, your FUTURE EMPLOYER.

Note to the company lawyers before you sue me: There may be great internships at the Mayo Clinic, Apple, and Boeing. The point here is to evaluate the specific internships before accepting one and not be hypnotized by the positive reputation of the corporate brand.

Negative Reason Two: Resume Building

Refer to the previous note. In this day and age, employers generally don't care who your employer was. They want to know what skills you acquired wherever you were.

Negative Reason Three: Friends

Your best friend just got a great internship at General Electric. But while the skills they will be getting are important for their career path, you are not convinced the skills on this internship will be as important for yours. Take a pass.

Negative Reason Four: Boredom

Your grades are so good you don't need summer courses or financial help? Interview until you find a position matching one of the positive reasons previously noted.

The Internship Agreement

One of the great things about hiring interns through Drexel University's Internship Office is that in addition to the normal "help wanted" job description, they require descriptions of both the intern's job duties and what they will learn.

While "fetching coffee" and "running errands" may be acceptable for an internship on the Howard Stern radio program (as described on air by one of his interns), such a description would probably be tossed into the trash for a STEM internship accepted by the Drexel office. (By the way, that is in no way a slam on the King of Media. I am a fan and understand the world of radio internships is different from the world of STEM internships.)

These descriptions enable prospective STEM interns from Drexel to be more intelligently selective about what position is the best fit for their situation. (Considering that for most positions, I've generally paid Drexel interns between two and four times minimum wage, having them do productive work is just good business practice.)

If you are considering an internship and are not completely clear about these topics, consider informing a prospective employer that you need such information in writing prior to accepting a position.

At any time during your internship, if it is clear you have been lied to and you are in fact a glorified coffee gofer, make your exit quickly and without apologies. While you don't want intentionally to burn any bridges, your time is too precious to waste on others who lack respect for it.

Harvard, MIT, and Cal-Tech – The Holy Trinity of STEM Schools [162]

College Reputation: Myths & Facts

There are more than 4,000 colleges in the United States. Poor choices of the one (or ones) that are most likely to benefit your STEM career are often the first steps on the road to failure. In this chapter, we will examine and blow up some of the existing college-choice rationales and point some of you in a much better direction.

Both in my generation and those of today, high school students choose their "first choice," "stretch choices," and "safe" colleges based often on perceived reputation. There are three rationales that support this logic. Unfortunately, the logic needs to be exposed as flawed and counterproductive for most STEM students.

Educational Quality

One rationale for this approach is that a school with a good reputation for a given major will give you a better education in that subject.

This is one reason that so many colleges trumpet the research accomplishments of their staff and base tenure offers and other honors and teacher benefits specifically on the volume of notable publications their teachers achieve.

This is also why most colleges keep their mouths shut about whether they fail fewer or the majority of their STEM students. Teaching competence and measures of teaching effectiveness often take a back seat to research and reputation building.

Employer Preference

There is another, complementary rationale for choosing your college based on reputation. That is the theory that graduating from a school with a better reputation (Johns Hopkins University, for example,) will get you hiring preference if your competition is from a lesser known school (such as Cooper Medical School of Rowan University).

In fact, this is often true. Some of the most competent people I have had the privilege of hiring and/or working with have been from MIT, Rensselaer, and Drexel. If I see a resume from someone from one of those three schools, I will at least read the resume.

Personally, I just want to know that the person has a degree from a properly accredited school in the right major and then I focus on their bulleted list of skills. I want to know how good a match the person is for the open position. As a result, I estimate that ninety-nine-point nine percent of the time, the reputation of the college has had no role at all in whom I interview or accept for a position.

Influential Lifetime Relationships

Development of influential lifetime relationships is a third rationale used to select colleges based on reputation. When you consider the socioeconomic classes and politically connected families behind many students at Harvard and Yale, it certainly makes sense to at least consider attending these schools if you are able.

Harvard, Yale, and to a slightly lesser degree, Princeton, produce not just doctors and lawyers, but future presidents and corporate and political leaders. While the quality of their courses may be similar to courses elsewhere, the social connections made by living at these schools are with the offspring of the country's political, media, and business elites. For the top one tenth of one percent of students, to turn down an opportunity to attend any of these three schools has traditionally been regarded as bordering on insanity.

In the world of business, a Wharton MBA has a similar reputation. In the world of technology, Cal Tech on the left coast and MIT on the right coast have reputations above all others.

Know that a tiny top percentage of students may have a valid rationale for choosing a school based not on the probability of educational success, but on reputation.

If you graduated in the top one percent of your high school class **and also** scored in the top one percent of the SATs (i.e. 2220 out of 2400), [13] then I am pretty comfortable you will survive the traditional four-year bachelor's schedule at five STEM courses per semester.

Now I'm going to address the remainder of those who graduated in the top half of their high school class and also scored in the top ten percent on their SATs. (i.e. at least a 1930 out of 2400).

It is for you that all manner of college ranking systems tend to distract you from choosing a school based on what should truly be most important (that is the odds of actually graduating).

US News and World Report magazine has long published annual rankings of colleges based on many criteria. Not to be outdone, there are now dozens of websites that try to help you understand the schools with the best reputations.

In 2015, Michigan State University's Professor Steve Hsu and Duke University's Jonathan Wai published an article that they attempted to rank colleges based on their contributions to science, society and technology. [6]

The colleges that they ranked are:

1.	Amherst College	20.	Princeton University
2.	Brown University	21.	Reed College
3.	Bryn Mawr College	22.	Rensselaer Polytechnic
4.	California Institute of		Institute
	Technology	23.	Rice University
5.	Carleton College	24.	Stanford University
6.	Carnegie Mellon	25.	Swarthmore College
	University	26.	University of California at
7.	Case Western Reserve		Berkeley
	University	27.	University of California at
8.	Columbia University		Los Angeles
9.	Cooper Union	28.	University of Chicago
10.	Cornell University	29.	University of Illinois at
11.	CUNY – City College of		Urbana-Champaign
	New York	30.	University of Michigan at
12.	Dartmouth College		Ann Arbor
13.	Harvard University	31.	University of Minnesota at
14.	Haverford College		Twin Cities
15.	Johns Hopkins University	32.	University of
16.	Massachusetts Institute of		Pennsylvania
	Technology	33.	University of Washington
17.	Oberlin College	34.	University of Wisconsin at
18.	Oregon State University		Madison
19.	Pomona College	35.	US Naval Academy
		36.	Wellesley
		37.	Yale University

(6)

(Interesting that of the colleges that I previously noted, only Cal Tech breaks into the top ten.)

But should any of this matter? For most of you, **it should not**.

What about the other ninety percent of aspiring college student? Again, most of this is but time-wasting distractions from identifying what school will truly give you the best odds for a well-paying job in the field of your choice.

So much of the media and college press is spent passionately (and sometimes desperately) to convince prospective students that their reputation is superior to their competition and that one should judge the quality of their education by their reputation.

Other schools do not even pretend they have the best reputation or education and will instead sell prospective students on school spirit, dorm maids, extra-curricular activities, or the quality of food in their cafeteria.

Rarely (ever?) will a school say, "Come here for the best chance at actually graduating into the career of your choice. (Attention readers. If you EVER run across such a school, please tell me at **www.thestemstudentsurvivalguide.com/feedback** with a link to their web site or any other source where they make this claim. As of 6/1/2016, I have yet to find more than the few that are noted in this book.)

So, as you consider selecting your college (or consider returning to college after failing out), this book will hopefully give you an arsenal of better questions to ask college representatives to increase your odds of successfully graduating.

Who Teaches?

I've already spent a lot of text beating up on colleges hiring and retaining teachers based on research and tenure priorities and not focusing on teaching abilities. This chapter explains the marketing pitch colleges give you and the real story behind who is actually teaching your classes.

So, you read the prior chapters and are not going to be swayed by spas and sushi. You go on your college tours and read up on the reputation of your prospective college.

You see the world-class research that builds the reputation of a college program you are interested in. Both the news articles and the college website provide glowing reviews of their professors.

You even are sure to exclude colleges who scam you by presenting lecture hall courses as suitable education.

Now is the time to ask the question about who in fact will be teaching those classes you are spending so much money for.

When you sign up for a specific college course, you rarely know in advance who is teaching, the history of how effective that teacher is in teaching the subject, or even the size of the class.

In selecting a doctor, a plumber, or a car manufacturer, there are all kinds of consumer information available, but not so with your college courses.

Instead, the student must rely on the college to control the quality of the course offering.

Just because my local hospital has a good reputation does not mean that I should allow the hospital to select the doctor who will be cutting me open. As a consumer, I get to select my doctor. But not at most colleges.

Just as you will be charged the same tuition for a class of 44 as a lecture hall course of 440, you will be charged the same amount of tuition regardless of who is teaching the course.

There are five different categories of teachers you may experience in the pursuit of your STEM degree. They are Full-Time Tenured Faculty, Full-Time Tenure-Track Faculty, Full-Time Non-Tenure Track Faculty, Part Time Faculty, and Graduate Student Employees.

Full-time Tenured Faculty

This is the stereotypical college professor. It is someone who almost always has earned a doctoral degree, had their research published, has established themselves as knowledgeable in their field, and been accepted by their peers and college administrators.

College administrators know that reputation is related to admissions and so achievements in their field may shadow any deficiencies as an educator. The achievement of tenure may or may not have any relationship to how effective that person is as a teacher.

According to a 2011 government survey, [46] only 17% of U.S. college teachers are Full-Time Tenured Faculty.

According to statistics on salary.com, [45] the median salary for a Professor of Mathematics is $96,821 that rises to $133,192 when benefits such as healthcare, paid vacation, and pension are added in.

If such a person teaches six courses a year in a public university with class sizes averaging 40 students, they will bring in between $250,000 and $500,000 in tuition revenue.

If such a person teaches through the summer and teaches 9 courses per year, each instructor may bring in between $350,000 and $700,000 per year in tuition revenue. (And this assumes zero lecture hall courses.)

However, while most tenured faculty are competent teachers, my experience and the experiences of many people I have talked to are that some are not. In most colleges, the administration will fill classes taught by tenured faculty prior to scheduling other instructors.

Due to the dual concepts of "academic freedom" and "tenure," many colleges find it almost challenging, and often impossible, to remove incompetent teachers from the classroom. If the student-customers had more market-place type abilities to choose their teachers, this would be less of an issue.

Full-time Tenure-Track Faculty

In every college, there are teachers whose hopes and dreams are to one day become a tenured teacher. However, for most of these people, the dream will stay a dream.

In a recent book, Andrew Hacker and Claudia Dreifus, an academic and a journalist, report that "America produced more than 100,000 doctoral degrees between 2005 and 2009. In the same period, there were just 16,000 new professorships." [50] In other words, 16% percent may have achieved their dream (assuming that zero percent of those who earned their doctorates prior to 2005 got any of those positions).

The odds are not quite as bad as buying a lottery ticket, but it is fascinating to see how many cling to their dream of tenure until the day they retire.

According to a 2011 government survey, [46] only 8% of U.S. college teachers are Full-Time Tenured Faculty.

Like their tenured brethren, the tenure-track individuals teach, but know they are judged mostly on their published research. So again, effective measurement of teaching effectiveness is not something that often gets the most attention.

In some colleges, tenure track faculty have a period of time in which to be approved for tenure. If tenure is denied, instead of continuing in the non-tenure role, they are often just fired to make room for the next tenure track person.

So, when you are taught by a tenure-track teacher, know that you are taught by someone who may be under-the-gun to produce stellar research and who may or may not very good at teaching.

Full-time, Non-Tenure Track Faculty

There are individuals who are not either not qualified or qualified, but not willing to take the risks associated with the pursuit of tenure. One might think that these people would be evaluated based on their teaching effectiveness. One would also frequently be wrong. These individuals make up about 15% of the college teachers nationwide.

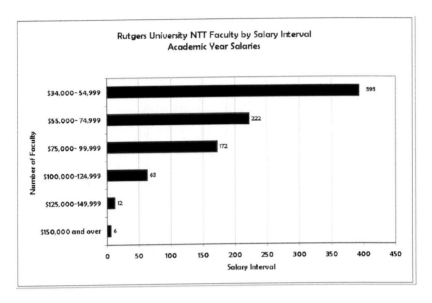

Rutgers University NTT Faculty by Salary Interval
Academic Year Salaries

Chart from the website of American Association of University Professors [73]

As Rutgers is a typical U.S. state college, let's take a look at how they compensate their Non-Tenure track Full Time teachers.

Of 868 Non-Tenure Track Full-Time Faculty at Rutgers, almost half are paid between $34,000 and $55,000. About a quarter are paid between $55,000 and $75,000. Most Rutgers classes are located in one of the highest cost-of-living areas in the country. [73]

In New Jersey, the median home price is $319,900. The median annual property taxes are $7,335. [75] As reported by USA Today [76], when the state's high-income tax is added, the cost of living in New Jersey is the second highest in the Nation and has been since at least 1977.

The reason for these statements? Your full-time non-tenure track college teacher is likely to either be working two jobs, or just stressed out about their finances. Need an assurance of teacher time outside of the classroom for personal help? Good luck.

Part Time Faculty

Now we have the largest percentage of the teachers you will experience. 41% of teachers nationwide are part-time faculty.
(46)

These are often individuals either working full time or retired. Sometimes, they are classified as "part time" employees or "adjunct faculty," even though all of their income may come from teaching.

Some have Master's degrees. More than 30,000 have Doctorates. [77] Many aspire for better compensation and rank as they teach the exact same classes as the tenured teachers.

However, most full time, Adjunct Faculty earn between $20,000 and $25,000 per year with no benefits.

Assume you were sick and could choose between two hospitals. One hospital had no particular reputation, but treated all their patients using full-time physicians whose only job was being a doctor. Another hospital had a reputation for employing a few world-famous physicians and had great food, but the patients had a 44% chance of being treated by a part-time doctor. Which hospital would you choose?

The health of your career may not be as important as your physical health, but it is important, none the less.

Graduate Student Employees

Graduate Students who are Teaching Assistants, comprise 19% of all college teachers. Across the US, the mean annual compensation for a Graduate Teaching Assistant is $32,000 annually. [78] The schools with better reputations do not necessarily pay more. For example, "A graduate assistant at Yale might earn $20,000 a year for nine months of teaching." [50]

Summary of United States Faculty Breakdown

Full-time Tenured Faculty 17%
Full-time Tenure-Track Faculty 8%
Full-time, Non-Tenure Track Faculty 15%
Part Time Faculty 41%
Graduate Students and others: 19%

According to a 2011 government survey, there are 1,846,895 faculty teachers in U.S. colleges.
[46]

A Bottom Line

You pay the same tuition for a "lecture hall" class of 400 as you do for a classroom of 40. You also pay the same tuition for a class taught by a tenured teacher whose total compensation for that class is $22,000 (times six for the six classes they teach for the entire year) as the 41% of classes taught by adjuncts who are paid between $3,000 and $4,000 for each class taught. No college I have yet researched discloses at the time of registration if the class will be taught by a graduate student (who may or may not have any skill at all in teaching).

A Second Bottom Line

It may not even matter if half or more of your teachers are lowly-paid adjuncts. Regardless of pay and rank, there are few (if any) objective measures that colleges use to insure the highest possible educational outcomes.

But the over-riding measure of the lack of success is clear. It is the 40% to 60% of STEM failures at most colleges.

Until there are independent prerequisite tests and independent post-course tests publicly available and tied to individual teachers; and until students can use that information to make informed course purchases; then it is college administrators who need to be held accountable for the miserable success rates experienced by their customers.

Sorry for such a dry chapter, but by now I'm hoping you will see through the "misinformation" [editor made me take out a curse word] that underlies a lot of what appear to be wonderful academic reputations.

Transfer Credit Limitations

(162)

Even if you think you will start and complete your bachelor's degree at only one college, life has a way of interrupting the best of plans.

Illness, low grades, job transfers, and unexpected financial challenges are some of the events that can require you to leave your original college.

Understanding how you may be able to assemble credits from multiple colleges into a single fully accredited degree may save you tens of thousands of dollars while also saving your sanity and career.

Even if you cannot imagine you will need this chapter, it may turn out to be the most valuable in the book.

Most colleges have policies that limit the number of credits they will accept for transfer from other colleges. While they may offer a lame excuse for doing so (controlling quality of their product), in fact the policies are focused on maximizing their income from each student.

There are also weird transfer rules on a per-college basis. Some will not transfer science credits older than four years, but will transfer liberal arts courses up to seven years. Some will accept an associate's degree no matter how old, but some will not.

These limitations are practices designed to maximize revenue to the granting college.

If this is likely to be an issue in your personal circumstance (for example, your work situation may require you to relocate one or more times during your college career), there are at least three fully accredited colleges who have thrived without limiting transfer credits.

For the financially thrifty, you can take courses online at the lowest possible cost and then either transfer those credits (or take advantage of Credit-by-Exam) to earn your fully accredited degree and emerge from college with little or no debt.

Those progressive institutions should be praised for their policies and more students should be aware of their options. Those colleges are Excelsior, Thomas Edison, and Charter Oak.

If you are part of the 40% to 60% of students abused by a conventional college, transferring courses taken as a full or part time student from one or many colleges to the three colleges I am about to praise may get you to that multi-million dollar paying career.

(Note that is repeated throughout this text: In the future, those colleges limiting the number of outside credits that they accept toward their diplomas should be required to disclose that for most majors, credits can be transferred to Excelsior College, Thomas Edison University, or Charter Oak University who award fully accredited diplomas without such limitations. If there is a popular major not offered by those colleges, then I advocate the government fund their expansion.)

Excelsior College
(excelsior.edu)

During your college tours, you may be given all kinds of excuses as to why the suggestions in the book are not workable. There are at least three colleges I've run across who provide at least part of the solution that I am lobbying for industry wide acceptance.

Let's start with some background about Excelsior College. Their trademarked philosophy is "what you know is more important than where or how you learned it. ®" [9]

Excelsior pioneered accredited online courses. They offer Credit by Exam. But most amazing of all, they do not limit in any way the number of credits you may transfer from other four-year schools toward your bachelor's degree and they do not limit the number of credits you may transfer from two-year schools toward your associates' degree. [9]

For example, if you have taken all of the necessary courses for a bachelor's degree, the cost for Excelsior to transfer the credits, evaluate your transcripts, and award you a bachelor's degree is less than $2,000.

Excelsior is a large, fully accredited college (both the college and their individual programs,) that offers a wide range of Associates, Bachelors, and Masters' degrees. Their nursing program alone has graduated more than 45,000 people since the 1970s. [9]

Excelsior's other STEM programs include Electrical Engineering (with concentrations offered in Electronics,

Nanotechnology, and Power Systems), Technology (with concentrations offered in Computer Technologies. Electromechanical Technologies, Electronic / Instrumentation Technologies, Nuclear Technologies, and Power Plant Technologies), and Health Sciences.

Excelsior's website explains their STEM programs fall into the following bachelor's programs:

- **Bachelor of Science in Cybersecurity:**
  - Bachelor of Science in Cybersecurity [Without Concentration]
  - Bachelor of Science in Cybersecurity (Operations)
  - Bachelor of Science in Cybersecurity (Health Care)

- **Bachelor of Science in Electrical Engineering Technology degrees:**
  - Bachelor of Science in Electrical Engineering Technology (Electronics)
  - Bachelor of Science in Electrical Engineering Technology (Nanotechnology)
  - Bachelor of Science in Electrical Engineering Technology (Power Systems)

- **Bachelor of Science in Information Technology degrees:**
  - Bachelor of Science in Information Technology [Without Concentration]
  - Bachelor of Science in Information Technology (Cybersecurity)
  - Bachelor of Science in Information Technology (Information Security)
  - Bachelor of Science in Information Technology (Network Operations)

- **Bachelor of Science in Nuclear Engineering Technology:**
  - Bachelor of Science in Nuclear Engineering Technology (Without Concentration)
  - Bachelor of Science in Nuclear Engineering Technology (Cybersecurity Technology)
  - Bachelor of Science in Nuclear Engineering Technology (Nuclear Leadership)

- **Bachelor of Professional Studies in Technology Management degrees:**

- Bachelor of Professional Studies in Technology Management (Electrical Technology)
- Bachelor of Professional Studies in Technology Management (Nuclear Technology)
- Bachelor of Professional Studies in Technology Management (Information Technology)
- Bachelor of Professional Studies in Technology Management (Renewable Energy Technology)

- **Bachelor of Science in Technology degrees:**
  - Bachelor of Science in Technology (Computer Technologies)
  - Bachelor of Science in Technology (Electromechanical Technologies)
  - Bachelor of Science in Technology (Electronic / Instrumentation Technologies)
  - Bachelor of Science in Technology (Nuclear Technologies)
  - Bachelor of Science in Technology (Power Plant Technologies)

While Excelsior's web site cost explanations are a little convoluted, their costs seem a little higher than Thomas Edison or Charter Oak.

If you are one of the thousands and thousands of students who earned some college credits but stopped or failed out, this is a college you should at least consider for your next adventure.

_____

Thomas Edison University
(tesu.edu)

Thomas Edison State University, is one of New Jersey's 11 public universities and colleges, offering degrees at the undergraduate and graduate level.

The college offers degrees at the undergraduate level, including seven associate degrees and 13 bachelor's degrees in more than 100 major areas of study. The university also offers 14 graduate degrees as well as undergraduate, graduate and noncredit certificates. [11]

The school and the school's programs are fully accredited.

More Wikipedia data:

* The school has been regionally accredited by the Middle States Commission on Higher Education since 1977.
* The W. Cary Edwards School of Nursing programs at Thomas Edison State University are approved by the New Jersey Board of Nursing, the Accrediting Commission for Education in Nursing (ACEN) and the Commission on Collegiate Nursing Education (CCNE).
* The Thomas Edison State University bachelor's degree programs in Electronic Systems Engineering Technology and Nuclear Energy Engineering Technology are accredited by the Engineering Technology Accreditation Commission of ABET. ABET is a specialized accrediting agency recognized by the Council for Higher Education Accreditation (CHEA).
[11]

According to the college's web site: [11]

The school's web site shows that they offer a wide variety of STEM degrees including

- Electronics Systems Engineering Technology
- Energy Systems Technology
- Health Services Technology
- Information Technology
- Nuclear Energy Engineering Technology
- Nuclear Engineering Technology
- Biomedical Electronics

On January 25th, 2017, I interviewed Bonnie Jean Gallagher, an admissions counselor for Thomas Edison State University (TESU). Bonnie was able to clarify some items that the web site covered and answered questions specific to this book.

First, as TESU accepts credits from all legitimate sources as defined in this book. Those courses do NOT "expire." Unlike many other colleges, even if that math course you took was taken five years ago, if you passed the course and remember the material, you will get full transfer credit and not have to retake the course. (However, you may desire to retake the course for personal refresher purposes. If you don't remember the material from Calculus I, you may be setting yourself up to fail Calculus II.).

TESU will accept up to 80 credits from regionally accredited community colleges, and up to 120 credits at regionally accredited four-year institutions.

TESU's online courses are taught in twelve-week semesters. Once admitted to the college, you only need to take one course every 12 months to remain an "active" student. This means if you work in retail or other industry where a busy season prevents you from taking a course, there is no problem in having a flexible schedule.

You may already have a bachelor's degree in an area that is not helping you. (For some people, Business or English?) In many cases your second bachelor's degree in an area more helpful to your career may be earned with only 24 more credits.

If you don't know if you have the discipline to be an online student, there are several options to find out. First, there is no charge to take a "test drive" course found on the TESU web site.

As a non-matriculated student, courses are offered at $525 per credit, which is a tiny fraction of the cost at most four-year and five-year schools.

Assuming you apply to be accepted as a matriculated student, out-of-state residents pay $499 per credit hour and New Jersey Residents pay $385 per hour.

While the above prices are for 2017 course, the savings difference between TESU courses and state and private colleges are expected to keep TESU a high-quality bargain.

Technically, TESU wants you to complete at least 16 credits as part of their "residency requirement." Don't fret. If you complete your 120-credit bachelor's degree without those 16 credits, TESU will waive the residency requirement after you pay $2,000 for a "residency waiver."

The only course a TESU student absolutely must take at TESU is a one-credit $300 online course "designed to assess their readiness in areas relevant to student success."

Whether you take your courses at public and/or private colleges, and whether those courses are taken in the classroom or online, TESU is the college I endorse and recommend above all others as your "safety valve" to insure you receive credit for your achievements and an accredited degree for your efforts.

Disclosure:

I have not been offered nor have I ever accepted financial compensation from ANY college for my endorsement. I endorse TESU because they appear to be the best choice for many people who have taken courses at one or more other courses and need a way to be legitimately rewarded for their efforts.

I may, from time-to-time teach a course at any college noted in this book. (As of this writing, I have not taught at any ANY college noted in this book.)

If I ever DO teach somewhere, I may or may not also recommend that college for the reasons noted in this book.

To sum up this chapter, TESU shows that Excelsior is not the only progressive college in the marketplace.
(10) (11)

Charter Oak State College
(charteroak.edu)

Charter Oak State College (COSC) is a public liberal arts college in New Britain, Connecticut. The college offers associate, bachelor's, and master's degrees. COSC is one of 17 higher learning institutions that comprise Connecticut State Colleges and Universities (ConnSCU). It is regionally accredited by the New England Association of Schools and Colleges, and functions under the degree-granting authority of the Connecticut Board of Regents for Higher Education. Charter Oak has awarded over 11,000 degrees since its founding in 1973.

From the Charter Oak website:

"Charter Oak has two academic residency requirements. The first is a 3-credit cornerstone course required for students enrolled in either an associate or bachelor's degree program at the college. The cornerstone course is taken in the student's first term as an enrolled Charter Oak student. The second is a 3-credit capstone course required of all students completing a bachelor's degree."

"Charter Oak has a liberal credit transfer policy. We will accept most credits that have been successfully completed at other regionally accredited institutions. This includes up to 87 semester credits from regionally accredited, two-year colleges. Exceptions include courses in physical education, freshman orientation, and developmental courses. Please visit How to Apply to apply online and begin your credit evaluation."

(12)

I called Charter Oak college to inquire how many Bachelor's level credits they will accept for transfer. On June 3, 2016, Mary Ruiz of the registrar's office confirmed they accept up to 87 transfer credits from 2-year schools and there is no limit on transfer credits from 4-year schools.

According the Charter Oak's website (charteroak.edu), the Bachelor degree programs offers as of January, 2017 are:

Business Administration
Cyber Security
Health Care Administration
Health Information Management
Psychology
General Studies, with these concentrations:
American Studies
Child and Youth Development
Child Studies
Criminal Justice
Human Resources
Information Systems Studies
Organizational Leadership
Paralegal Studies
Political Science
Public Administration
Public Safety Administration
Sociology

For the purposes of this book, Charter Oak only has a few STEM majors. They are Cyber Security, Health Care Administration, Health Information Management, and Psychology.

The per-credit costs are less than those at Thomas Edison.

If Charter Oak offers you a program not offered by Thomas
Edison, this college should be on your short list of resources to
help you get your accredited degree.

For-Profit College Warning

Once in a while, I am researching a topic and run across an
article that explains the situation so much better than I think I
can. Here is a lightly edited 2014 article by Lindsay Haskell that
contains information you should have before accepting a
relationship with a for-profit college. (The article applies to
ALL majors, so understand the STEM statistics are probably
much worse.)

---

(38) For profit college dropout and compensation article

SEPTEMBER 20TH 2014 By: Lindsay Haskell
http://www.attn.com/stories/118/graduation-rate-profit-colleges-
shocking

The Graduation Rate of For-Profit Colleges is Shocking....

For-profit colleges (think University of Phoenix or ITT Tech)
are coming under intense scrutiny by the federal government
and the public alike - and for good reason. Many exploit
students, especially those from low income backgrounds, for
tuition money with no guaranteed return-on-investment in
terms of acquired skills or job opportunities.

While a key appeal of for-profit colleges is that
they accommodate flexible schedules, this perk does not
begin to make up for their failings.

- Only 22 percent of full-time students seeking a Bachelor's
  degree graduate, compared to 55% at public institutions
  and 65% at private nonprofits.

- Sadly, those who manage to obtain a degree do not fare much better: 72% of for-profit colleges produce graduates that earn less than high school dropouts.

And despite these bleak prospects, many students are paying more tuition than they would at other universities. The average tuition at a for-profit college is six times higher than a community college and twice as high as a public four-year school. To fund this education, 96% of for-profit students take out loans, which then haunt them after college.

- More for-profit college graduates default on their student loans than other graduates (21.8 percent compared to 13 percent at public universities and 8.2 percent at private nonprofit colleges).
- Despite accounting for only 11% of federal loan borrowers, for-profit students comprise nearly 50% of loan defaulters.

The business models of for-profit schools are also quite dubious. Roughly 86% of their revenue comes from federal aid. And where is their other profits coming from? Why, GI Bills, of course. In 2012 alone, one of the largest for-profit college companies, Corinthian Colleges, received $186 million in post-9/11 GI Bill funds. So by targeting lower income families and veterans, for-profit colleges gets the federal government to guarantee the tab with loans, GI bills, and grant programs (the Pell Grant alone constituted $7.9 billion for these institutions in 2010), that come out to roughly $33 billion a year. It's no wonder, then, that the 15 largest for-profit colleges chose to spend $3.7 billion (23% of their budget) on advertising and marketing in 2009 alone, compared to non-profit schools which only put 1% of their budget towards advertising. [38]

The article continues to explain how the colleges have various politicians in their pockets, but that is not relevant for this book. The bottom line here is to be extremely cautious before engaging with any of the for-profit colleges.

Gap Year Data and Benefits

Jean Piaget was one of the most influential psychologists of the twentieth century. By the end of the 20th century, Piaget was second only to B. F. Skinner as the most cited psychologist of that era. [66]

Piaget not only identified how individuals progressed through different stages of development, but that perfectly normal people mature at different rates, completing various stages at different ages.

Recently, there has been a substantial amount of discovery about the development and maturation of the brain. For many people (especially males), brain maturity is a process that does not complete until sometime in their twenties. [63] [64] [65] Yet the vast majority of STEM students are male and in the US, almost all start college three months after graduating from high school.

I recently spoke with Jordan, a young lady who was entering her last year of Drexel University's five-year Civil Engineering program. Jordan confirmed that the vast majority of Drexel engineering students were male and half or more failed out or changed to non-STEM majors during their first two years of school. She also observed that a high percentage of Drexel STEM students are foreign, are male, and seem to have a much lower failure rate than their American counterparts.

This was especially fascinating as students from the countries with the best Math and Science programs (such as Finland, Norway, and Sweden), are coming from countries that traditionally have shorter high school days and much less homework than found in U.S. schools.

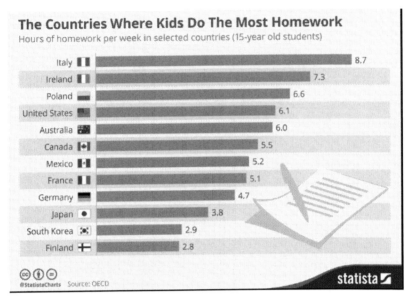

The Countries Where Kids Do The Most Homework
Hours of homework per week in selected countries (15-year old students)

Italy	8.7
Ireland	7.3
Poland	6.6
United States	6.1
Australia	6.0
Canada	5.5
Mexico	5.2
France	5.1
Germany	4.7
Japan	3.8
South Korea	2.9
Finland	2.8

@StatistaCharts   Source: OECD   statista

(116)

In comparison, the American high school students generally are used to five-hour school day to the Finland's four-hour school day.

There is a difference between many foreign students and their American counterparts. The difference is that sometimes European students take one or more years to work or travel between high school and college. This is sometimes called the "gap year." (118)

In fact, there is an organization appropriately named, The American Gap Association, (AGA,) (http://www.americangap.org) that advances "the field of Gap Years by collaboratively pioneering research on its benefits, as well as serving as an information and advocacy hub for university admissions personnel and educational counselors."
(62)

According to the AGA website,

""Some studies have looked at the academic performance of gap year students while in college. In Australia and the United Kingdom, economic researchers found that high school students who deferred their admission to college to take a Gap Year went to college (after their Gap Year) at the same rate as those who accepted an offer and intended to go straight there (Birch and Miller 2007; Crawford and Cribb 2012). They also found that taking a Gap Year had a significant positive impact on students' academic performance in college, with the strongest impact for students who had applied to college with grades on the lower end of the distribution (Birch and Miller 2007; Crawford and Cribb 2012)." In fact, in the United Kingdom and in the United States, students who had taken a Gap Year were more likely to graduate with higher grade point averages than observationally identical individuals who went straight to college, and this effect was seen even for Gap Year students with lower academic achievement in high school (Crawford and Cribb 2012, Clagett 2013)."

(62)

My personal values are to embrace the Scientific Method. That is, I need to be open to ideas that do not fit into my personal experiences if those ideas are backed up by objective evidence. Most of this book is devoted to the idea that the high percentage of STEM failures are due to education system incompetence, and not related to the students themselves.

After reviewing the GAP study, I gave some thought to the experiences of my own family members. Both of my daughters are highly intelligent people who became self-sufficient adults at a very young age. When each decided to "take a break" after high school, I found myself aggravated and was convinced that they were making colossal mistakes. I have a number of friends who "took time off" after high school, never completed college, and experienced decades of low paying jobs they generally do not enjoy. My advice to "tough it out" and go straight to college was ignored by each daughter.

As I write this sentence, one daughter has a bachelor's degree which she earned with top grades from beginning to end. The other daughter now has bachelor's and master's degrees and is currently studying for her Ph.D. on a full scholarship. It was a good thing that my daughters ignored my advice. They each knew when they were ready for college. Unlike the title of the 1950s TV show, sometimes, "father does NOT know best."

The problem here is that we have no metric that measures brain maturity, or maturity related to self-sufficiency when it comes to admitting college students.

One problem with my even noting this issue in the book is that some college administrators will exaggerate the level of this issue to once again blame their customers. Elsewhere in the book, I give an example of how one college increased their student pass rate to 87% without offering the option of taking a GAP year. They did this by implementing some more progressive teaching techniques in the classroom and by formalizing tutoring and support outside of class.

I suggest a slightly different approach. If you truly want to increase the odds of STEM college success, then first ask yourself if a GAP year is appropriate for your circumstances. If so, then great. If not, then consider a "ramp up" schedule where the first semester, you take only two courses, and even then, only one "Weeder" course. Then increase your "dosage" of courses, one per semester according to the plan you select from an earlier chapter.

If your first or second semester is a total disaster, then consider a GAP year. Even if you only have a low-paying job for that year, it may be the period where your brain finally matures and your brain chemistry and related hormones finally calms down.

Wrapping Up the Chapters Thus Far

The bottom line message of all the text so far: Our STEM educational system is broken, but survivable. The financial rewards and career satisfaction is worth the aggravation. You can take actions to reduce your stress. **<u>And yes, you can emerge with an accredited degree with tolerable debt.</u>**

If you were in the top third of your high school class and top quarter of those taking the SAT or ACT exams, and then chose to study in a STEM program:

- You may now be planning a STEM education.
- You may now already be struggling through a STEM education.
- You may have already failed at one or more attempts at a STEM education.

In any of these scenarios, the previous pages should have provided you with one or multiple strategies to regroup and this time successfully succeed in your STEM mission.

If you are part of the population of people who have graduated from a STEM program, how many of your friends could have benefitted from this advice?

SHAMELESS PLUG

If your loved ones, or other friends are failing or have already failed out of a STEM program, buy them this book. It could get them back in school and onto a better path!

(162)

To buy this book in print or electronic form, please consider purchasing directly from my website at

www.TheSTEMStudentSurvivalGuide.com

and I will earn a few extra dollars from the sale.

Also, if you would like to sign up for my email list (once a month or less and I will not sell your address to others,) the web address is the same.

This ends the portion of the book containing strategies students can use right now to succeed in today's environment.

The pages that follow are targeted to lawmakers, regulators, and college administrators. They explain how they may improve the stress and misery that students and their families (who are, after all, their customers,) currently suffer.

Chapters for College Administrators, Lawmakers, and Regulators

For College Administrators

If you got this far in the text, you know that I am not a fan of many current practices common in many colleges. That said, I understand that rather than being evil mutants who have no regard for your customers, that most of you are trapped in a system where outside competitive practices seem to force you into acting as cogs in the machine that chews up and spits out between 40% and 60% of your STEM students.

(Yes, I know there are some exceptions like MIT who gets to select the top 1% of potential students based on SATs and class rank. I am referring to the great majority of STEM colleges who have no such luxury.)

What I will be proposing in this chapter are steps for you to consider implementing to "get ahead" of the coming legislative and policy changes advocated in subsequent chapters. Now is the time to plan.

The current environment builds college reputations based on name recognition (therefore the importance of college athletics), research publicity (therefore the importance of college ratings), and comforts (therefore the importance of investing in resort-quality amenities for impressive college tours).

With a little help from the government and media, this should change over time.

When one purchases a mortgage today, there are a number of pages of disclosure that the consumer is provided by law and regulation. [130] From actual interest rates to various fees paid to different parties, the consumer is now provided with much better information than experienced by past generations.

The day is coming when different metrics will be presented to the students who are your customers. If the lobbying advocated later in this book is successful, there will be financial consequences as colleges with high fail out rates experience declines in enrollment and funding.

I do not expect all of the recommendations in this book will be implemented nor do I expect the transition will be rapid. But when the changes do come, they may seem rapid and consequential to those colleges and teachers who are not prepared.

Relationship Issues & Priorities

The classic science fiction film, "2001, A Space Odyssey," and its sequel "2010: The Year We Make Contact," tell a story of conflicting values. In the first film, when astronauts decide to abort their mission, the very computer that was programmed to protect their lives, embarks on an astronaut killing spree. In the second film, it was explained that the computer had a second, secret program, which instructed it not to let anything interfere with the mission. As a result of having conflicting goals, the computer made some pretty questionable decisions.

In a less dramatic manner, colleges and college administrators are faced with multiple responsibilities that sometimes seem to conflict with each other. In serving some of these responsibilities, decisions are sometimes made that conflict with other responsibilities.

Only by recognizing these conflicts can we start to remediate some of the consequences arising from those conflicts. While no one dies as a result of these conflicts, STEM students are often bankrupted and/or dispirited, and society is deprived of the services of those who fail.

Let's start by reviewing the five highest priorities facing college administrators:

1. Maintaining Fiscal Solvency
2. Advocating for Teacher Interests
3. Facilitating Research
4. Facilitating Other Community Interests
5. Advocating for Student Interests

1. Maintaining Fiscal Solvency

The highest priority of any college must be fiscal solvency. A college that spends more money than can be offset by revenue from various sources will eventually close. With limited funds to spend, college administrators are forced to make a number of less-than-desirable budgetary decisions every year.

Full-time staff are expensive. That is why the majority of teachers are now part-timers who are poorly compensated compared to their full-time peers performing the same teaching tasks. It is also why administrators continue to fill lecture halls with hundreds of students per class, despite abysmally high failure rates.

Recruiting students is highly competitive. That is one reason why colleges are keen to fund highly visible research, athletic programs, spas, and gourmet food options. Funds spent in these areas decrease funds available for teacher salaries and smaller classrooms.

For most institutions, maintaining accreditation is a necessary prerequisite to retaining both teachers and students. As a result, policies and assets required to maintain accreditation drive required expenditures.

While all of the other following priorities are important, maintaining fiscal solvency trumps all other considerations.

2. Advocating for Teacher Interests

The actual business of a college is the delivery of education and research to those who are fund the education and research. The actual delivery is provided for the most part, by teachers. (That is not to disregard the contributions of all the other staff who work for the college, but to note that in the final analysis, the teacher provides the actual education and research.)

To recruit and retain teachers costs money. There are some who may maintain that the majority of teachers are neither overpaid nor underpaid. Instead, they might argue that the supply of teachers and the demand for those hiring teachers is a marketplace like any others. Just as plumbers, painters, and medical doctors charge no more than what the market offers to pay for their services, so too will some argue that as there are many more applicants than there are positions, that the compensation offered to teachers is probably sufficient.

There are, in my view, flaws in the above argument. First, that the STEM-related educational services offered by colleges are NOT meeting the needs of many paying customers. Not only do teachers need the necessary incentives to improve the quality of the teaching product, but they also need sufficient compensation to spend more time with those students who are failing to master the necessary material.

Until between 95% and 99% of the paying customers are able to master the required material, it is possible that schools may not be investing sufficient funds in teacher compensation. I am open to reviewing evidence that better results can be achieved by the existing mixture of full-time and part-time resources. But as of the time this text was written, it looks to me like schools are underpaying for resources and not being held accountable for their delivering of miserable results.

There are some teachers whose main passion is research. There are some teachers whose main passion is teaching. There is some percentage of teachers competent in both areas. Based on current results, it appears that American colleges deliver stellar research and hideous educational outcomes for about half of all STEM students.

I believe it is time to separate educational budgets from research budgets and that teaching compensation and incentives be separated from research compensation and incentives.

Proposed Teacher Compensation Approach

From the perspective of the student as a consumer, today's approaches to teacher compensation make no sense. The majority of teachers are not full-time instructors and are paid meagerly. (I guess I should not complain as the pay is rarely related to objective measures of educational outcomes.) From a business perspective, colleges are incented to pay their teachers as little as possible, regardless of the quality of service provided to their students. In addition, the pressure to keep wages low results in limited teacher availability outside of class time, and incentivizes quantity of classroom teaching hours over quality.

To appropriate a catchphrase from motivational speaker, nutritionist, personal trainer, and author, Susan Powter, we need to "Stop the Insanity."

This chapter proposes a baseline approach. It can certainly be tweaked and revised as better market-based approaches and supporting data are developed.

I start my proposal with the assumption that properly compensated and incented full-time teachers will be able to spend the time necessary (in and out of the classroom) to ensure that at LEAST 90% of their students are able to pass a post-course independent final exam that demonstrates mastery of all required material.

The Benefits Portion of Compensation

As reported by Salary.com, [45] Professor of Mathematics in the Philadelphia area, 37% of median compensation is in the form of benefits. This translated to $36,371 of benefit value. (See illustration.)

Let us assume that a college adopts a true "trimester" approach where the "summer" semester courses are at least 10 to 12 weeks in duration. This would imply that teachers are available to teach nine courses per year.

Professor - Mathematics PHILADELPHIA, PA

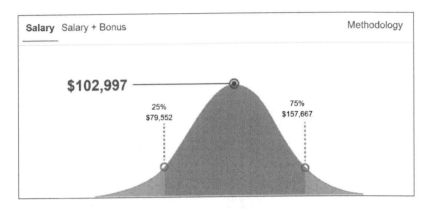

| Salary Salary + Bonus | | Methodology |

Core Compensation	Median	% of Total
Base Salary	$102,997	72.9%
Bonuses	$0	0.0%
Value of Benefits		
Social Security	$7,879	5.6%
401K/403B	$3,708	2.6%
Disability	$927	0.7%
Healthcare	$6,592	4.7%
Pension	$6,489	4.6%
Time Off	$12,677	9.0%
Total Compensation	**$141,269**	**100%**

Chart: [45]

To prevent colleges from being incented to substitute part-time labor who generally do not have as much time available to work with their students outside of the classroom, I suggest that accreditation require that for every course taught by a teacher without benefits, that the college be required to pay a "benefits stipend" of $4,041 for each course taught ($36,371 divided by 9 courses). This would enable the faculty without benefits to pay for their own health care, retirement, and so on. The "benefits stipend" is separate and additional to the actual salary paid to the teacher for teaching the course.

Divorcing Research from Teaching

When I speak about teaching compensation, I mean just that. Colleges should segregate funds raised for and spent on research from funds raised for and spent on teaching. If a teacher is expected to spend 50% of their times (about 900 hours per year) on research, then their paycheck should have separate line items for research compensation and teaching compensation.

I pay taxes to the government so the government can fund research. Corporations and foundations also fund a portion of college research. If I am paying tuition for myself or my kids, I want to pay for education, thank you very much. If a college has an endowment, I propose the endowment be split into a fund for education and a separate fund for endowment and where the money is spent be made very public.

Tying Compensation to Educational Outcomes

By implementing the various approaches suggested in this book, there is no reason that successful outcomes of between 90% and 99% cannot be expected and achieved.

We know from salary.com that the base salary range for a Philadelphia-based Professor of Mathematics ranges from $54,708 to $195,032 with a median salary of $96,821. (These figures do not include benefits.)

I would suggest that for teachers where 80% of their students pass an independent post-course mastery exam, that the salary portion of their compensation be awarded at $10,758 ($96,821 divided by 9 courses per year).

For every percentage point above 80%, they should receive a 2% bonus until 90% percent of their students achieve mastery. In other words, if 90% of their students pass the final, then their compensation would include a bonus" of 20%. This amount would be their incentive to work with students outside of class time is appropriate.

For every percentage point above 90%, the bonus would be another 5%. In other words, any time a teach is able to work with and pass 100% of their students, their compensation for that course would be $18,305. Remember that I previously advocated for final exams administered by the department and developed by national committees, not the teacher. This would prevent grade inflation and guaranty that grades reflect real learning.

How do we get rid of those teachers who cannot teach? Enabling students to choose their teachers is one solution that empowers the student as a responsible consumer.

Ensuring that taxpayers are compensated for the likely loan defaults caused by incompetent teachers is another approach.

I suggest that for any course where the final mastery rate as measured by an independent test is less than 80%, that the teacher's compensation be reduced by 2% for each percentage point below 80%. In other words, a class with a 70% pass rate would pay 20% less than the $10,758 base. A class with a 60%

pass rate would pay 40% less than the $10,758 base. And so forth.

Assuming no student is accepted into a class without passing the pre-test, this system provides both rewards and accountability.

As the suggested system is based on objective measures, it is not based on politics or personality.

Some college administrators might object to this entire discussion. Teacher compensation is not the business of an outsider, they might say. If they make this argument, then I will make the argument that the college needs to be held responsible for the quality of their product and be required by law to refund the tuition of all the students that fail a course (and where the final exam is administered by an impartial outside organization).

Come to think of it, each college should be given an option. Either they take responsibility for their product and have to refund the failures, or they delegate the responsibility to the students who are their customers and need the power to purchase or not purchase a course based on publicized performance of that teacher teaching that course.

If that ever happens, we will experience a rapid and dramatic change to college priorities and practices.

3. Facilitating Research

Many colleges pride themselves on conducting research as one of their prime missions. Unfortunately, the emphasis on research has allowed the development of a culture that does not focus on educational outcomes.

This is one of the reasons I am advocating so strongly for a separation of funding and accounting for time spent on research as opposed to time spent delivering education.

4. Facilitating Other Community Interests

While research is the most common non-educational service, there are others. From operating hospitals to operating high schools and from bringing cultural performances to neighborhoods, to conducting national polls and amateur sports, there are a host of activities that are often justified as reputation builders that will help recruit more customers.

However, as the public focus finally starts to shift to educational outcomes, I expect a little more scrutiny may be given as to which of these other interests are really in the customers' best interest.

5. Advocating for Student Interests

So here we have finally arrived at the fifth, last, and lowest priority, the students who are theoretically the college's customers.

It is in the student's interest to be guided to the college that most increases the odds of the student successfully graduating as a competent member of their desired profession and with the least amount of debt possible.

But as the college needs to place their own financial solvency as their highest priority, every college pretends that they and they alone are the best choice for the students they accept.

Even though the college will not disclose the performance record of individual teachers.

Even though the college will gloss over any deficiencies in class size.

Even though the college will limit the ability of students to take less expensive courses elsewhere and transfer those credits.

(Have I beaten these concepts to death? Have I achieved maximum reader aggravation?)

The "Government Actions" chapter of the book, I include a proposal that colleges realize they have a fiduciary duty to guide students as a result of legislation codifying that responsibility. It is time right now to prepare for that eventuality.

Teachers and Teaching Practices

In this book, I have been critical of the existing educational system, including current practices and policies. However, I have not been all that critical of the teachers themselves. This is because I am convinced that with a combination of the proper incentives and measures of accountability, the vast majority of teachers who need to change their teaching practices will do so.

The causes for my optimism are both subjective and objective. For subjective experience, one of my most knowledgeable resources is my daughter, Skye, who taught for eight years at Prescott College before moving to SUNY Albany to pursue her doctorate. Skye's observations have been that while good teachers are valued by college administrators, that good researchers are often valued a great deal more. I have had the fortune of meeting many college teachers, both adjunct and tenured, and count at least one high-level college administrator as a dear friend.

EVERY ONE of the teachers I have met are caring and intelligent people who are open to fixing the deficiencies in the system. This includes those teachers who judge their failing students as either too dumb or too lazy or insufficiently prepared, as the reasons for their failures. While this may not be a large enough sample to speak for the universe of all teachers, I am greatly encouraged.

With regard to my own education, of the more than 60 college courses I have taken (both under-graduate and graduate,) I ran across no more than three teachers who seemed to me to be truly incompetent or at the very least indifferent to the needs of their students.

That does not mean the 95% of the remainder of the teachers used all the methods necessary to ensure that the majority of their students mastered the subject material. It just means that based on my observations, that they would have no problem using such methods if they were trained, measured, and suitably compensated for using those methods.

Based on those subjective observations, my issue is with the system that molds and manages these teachers, not the teachers themselves.

For my one of my objective reasons for being optimistic, I point to recent approaches that have improved the quality of medical practices in the United States.

Whether correct or not, doctors are often thought to be individuals who are resistant to changing the way they practice medicine. However, a recent Wall Street Journal Article (June 26th, 2016, "To Get Doctors to Do the Right Thing, Try Comparing Them to Their Peers,") by Laura Landro, shows the success that results when doctors are aware they are being compared to others. [68] The following excerpts and edited restatements are drawn from that article:

> Healthcare organizations would like to improve how doctors follow up on test results in order to make the correct diagnosis and select the right treatment.
>
> One such goal is the reduction of unnecessary prescription of antibiotics despite clear guidelines that those drugs should only be used to fight bacterial infections and not for viral infections such as the flu. "A recent Pew Charitable Trusts report concluded that 30% of antibiotic prescriptions are unnecessary, or nearly 47 million excess prescriptions a year." The results of the

current practices are the rise of antibiotic resistance, increased healthcare costs, and increased medical incidents of patients who suffer from reactions to their medications.

In a study published in February in JAMA doctors received monthly reports about their prescribing habits and how they compared to their peers. Those doctors who failed to be noted as "top performers" changed their bad prescribing habits and overall unwarranted prescriptions fell from 20% to 4% during the study. [68]

It is time for colleges to publicize the percentage of STEM students who fail to master a course subject not by the college or department, but by individual teachers. After all, the college does not teach a course. The student purchases a course to be taught by an individual instructor. As the consumer, students should be free to purchase their courses only as empowered and educated consumers.

Those colleges with competent administrators would see them stand up to the unions and remove the incompetent teachers from the classroom.

To prevent "grade inflation," course mastery can be measured by final exams offered by the department or authorities independent of the college.

By embracing this very basic empowerment of the college customer, other changes to policies and practices will fall into place as tuition money will be steered to those teachers and institutions who offer better instruction for the tuition dollar.

There will be some colleges and teachers who traditionally offer their services to students from challenged backgrounds who will scream that this approach discriminates against them. To address their concerns, colleges should consider a "Pre-requisite Exam" for most STEM courses. A student whose Prerequisite Exam grade does not demonstrate MASTERY of the subject should be channeled into remedial courses until they are truly ready for the course in question. If both students and teachers are graded on the educational outcome, then both will be accountable for delivering successful results.

In fact, certain teachers who are dedicated and skilled instructors will quickly be identified. Imagine what happens when a college can advertise that their instructors enable 90% or more of their students to achieve MASTERY of all required material.

The marketplace will quickly shift as students will opt to spend their dollars more wisely. It is no coincidence that as consumer publications rate reliability of certain automobile manufacturers to be superior, that the market slowly but surely rewarded those manufacturers. Just as impressive, as the manufacturers of lower quality ranked automobiles experience declining market share in the 1970s and 1980s, those that could improve their product (such as Ford) eventually increased their sales and market share, while those who could not (such as American Motors and Yugo) have been relegated to the dust bin of history.

In a market where teaching quality by teacher is public knowledge and students have power over where their dollars are spent, colleges will pursue the best teachers with six figure compensation packages instead of pursing stadiums, spas, and sushi.

For colleges who spend their money on stadiums and sushi bars instead of top quality professors, economist Adam Smith's "invisible hand" used to describe the unintended social benefits of individual actions, should lead to the survival of colleges who actually deliver the best educational results. [71]

Proof That Better Results are Possible

There are many dedicated teachers whose STEM research is focused on how to improve the outcomes of STEM classes.

In 2016, Karen Shakerdge authored an article for The Hechinger Report showing how modifying some traditional approaches to classroom instruction raised pass rates from 50% to 80%. [80] (And that is without any of the other suggestions contained in the first 100 pages of this book!)

The fact that some teachers and colleges are succeeding at teaching STEM courses tells me that the remainder are either focusing their attention and priorities elsewhere, or just don't care.

Here are excerpts and edited restatements are drawn from Ms. Shakerdge's article:

> At San Diego State University, teaching assistant Natalie Nowicki's Calculus II class is taught differently from conventional math classes. It starts with the layout of desks which face each other in small groups instead of the traditional orientation toward the teacher or the board.
>
> Students are given a worksheet to consider in each small group. Ms. Nowicki then asks each group to explain their reasoning. Rather than a lecture, the students are engaged in a discussion where their attention is focused on the topic.
>
> This is part of several new approaches implemented in 2014. At that time, Michael O'Sullivan, chair of the math and

statistics department, worked with department faculty to address the problem that between 35 and 50 percent of students in all math courses were either earning a D, an F, or just withdrawing from each course.

They "extended class hours, established a learning center and "learning communities" to offer support for students who typically struggle in math and science classes."

In their approach, students continued to attend lectures. However, they also started attending small group sessions focused on "student-centered active learning," in which the focus would be on concept-based discussion — not just absorbing information. The smaller sessions are required and match the material taught in the lectures.

The teachers at San Diego State University are not the only ones trying newer approaches. At the University of Nebraska-Lincoln (UNL), class time was extended, teaching assistants were trained in active-learning techniques, and the tables were rearranged into groups. As a result, the student pass rate for math courses over time rose from 62 percent to 80 percent where it remains today.

Scott Freeman, a biology instructor at the University of Washington, studied the impact of active learning techniques. He and co-investigators found that, on average, these techniques raise the pass rate from 66 percent to almost 80 percent for STEM course. [80]

The examples of these successes have been studied and validated many times. In fact, Sandra Hines of the University of Washington reviewed more than 200 studies of similar practices in her article "Improve grades, reduce failure – undergrads should tell profs 'Don't lecture me.'" [82]

Ms. Hines reviewed the work of Scott Freeman, a University of Washington principal lecturer in biology.

> "Freeman and his co-authors based their findings on 225 studies of undergraduate education across all of the "STEM" areas: science, technology, engineering and mathematics. They found that 55 percent more students fail lecture-based courses than classes with at least some active learning." [82]

> "On average across all the studies, a little more than one-third of students in traditional lecture classes failed – that is, they either withdrew or got Fs or Ds, which generally means they were ineligible to take more advanced courses. On average with active learning, a little more than one-fifth of students failed." [82]

With every example of a college with high STEM retention rates, the case becomes stronger that the rest need to improve or face consequences.

At Perdue University, the traditional experience was that "sixty percent of freshman engineering majors drop out or change majors." As of 2012, Perdue has implemented many progressive teaching approaches and "increased their freshman retention rate to 87% while maintaining their [existing] standards." [124]

Author Jon Marcus reviewed such schools in his 2012 web article, "High Dropout Rates Prompt Engineering Schools to Change Approach." [124]

Here are some observations drawn from Mr. Marcus' article:

Nationwide, forty percent of engineering students will drop out of their engineering programs in their first year of attendance. The number increases to sixty per cent when considering the second year.

"At the University of Colorado-Boulder, 300 freshmen engineering majors live together in dorms where the university offers free drop-in tutoring every weeknight, calculus work groups, and even late-night breakfasts before midterms. Eighty-six percent return for their sophomore years, versus 78 percent of freshmen who live elsewhere. At Washington University in St. Louis, students can get up to four hours a week of free one-on-one tutoring, or math counseling at a Calculus Help Room." [124]

If Purdue can achieve 87% retention before adopting the schedule stretching or advance tutoring, advocated earlier in this text, those schools that have a 50% dropout rate should be given notice to immediately improve or have their accreditations revoked.

What about Notre Dame?

On November 4th, 2011, a New York Times article about science majors noted that some colleges have experienced dramatic successes by implementing progressive approaches to teaching.

Notre Dame's engineering dean, Peter Kilpatrick, will be the first to concede that sophomore and junior years, which focus mainly on theory, remain a "weak link" in technical education. He says his engineering school has gradually improved its retention rate over the past decade by creating design projects for freshmen and breaking "a deadly lecture" for 400 students into groups of 80. Only 50 to 55 percent of the school's students stayed through graduation 10 years ago. But that figure now tops 75 percent, he says, and efforts to create more labs in the middle years could help raise it further. [122]

The New York Times at nytimes.com. Why Science Majors Change Their Minds (It's Just So Darn Hard). Author Christopher Drew.

How to Better Teach STEM Courses

For an example of how to better teach many "Weeder" courses, let us consider how calculus is taught today. An online scan of syllabi from a variety of colleges show very little difference in the course contents, topics, or approaches. Scanning the table of contents in multiple calculus textbooks on Amazon.com shows a near uniformity on what is being taught.

The typical college course consists of 45 classes over a 16-week college semester. (Three classes per week minus holidays.)

Subtract classes devoted to tests, test preparation, and other reviews and we are left with about 40 classes to deliver all of the topics required in Calculus I.

Let's contrast the more traditional approach with a more contemporary approach so we have a basis to improve both.

The traditional approach often divided a topic into three parts. First, a class lecture exposes the student to a new topic. Homework assignments enable the student to apply their new knowledge, and identify and resolve gaps in their understanding. Classroom discussion, question and answer, exercises, and quizzes then serve to cement the new knowledge prior to the next lecture.

In many contemporary environments, the lecture is replaced with a homework reading assignment and/or video lecture. Then, homework enables the student to try to apply their new knowledge. By doing this ahead of class, the student has the opportunity to identify gaps in prerequisite knowledge and also email the teacher with questions that might be addressed in class. The student also has the opportunity to reach out for help from peers, tutors, and sometimes the teacher.

The students may be given an online quiz prior to the class or in the first few minutes of class. If the quiz is graded in real-time, the teacher may immediately know what topics are challenging which students. In this case, the teacher may change the in-class discussions to address the needs of the class.

If the quizzes do not uncover any surprises, the teacher may lead class group discussions, answer questions, and then enable students or groups of students to engage in exercises.

The more contemporary approach often greatly increases homework with the goal of delivering a better educational result.

Depending on the college, the failure rate for Calculus I is still 30% or more, no matter which approach is used.

Arguing about which approach is better is analogous to rearranging the deck chairs on the Titanic after the iceberg has pierced the hull and the ship is quickly taking in water.

Let's back up and consider a different approach.

Imagine a college who is determined that all of their STEM students not just pass, but master the subject matter in Calculus I to ensure those same students will have the necessary competence when they subsequently register for Calculus II.

We'll start with the requirement that every student first takes an online national "Pretest." The sections of the Pretest will cover the topics necessary for teachers to be comfortable that the students have the prerequisite knowledge to enable them to subsequently not just pass the course, but to truly master the course material.

Imagine if the Pretest was divided into ten topics. (I'm being arbitrary here.) If the student fails even one of those topics, they would fail the exam even if their overall score was ninety per cent due to the fact that they had mastered all of the other topics.

Such a student would be placed in either a remedial math course, or, if they only failed a small number of topics, given tutoring until they passed the course.

The bottom line here is that if we are going to hold teachers accountable for success, we must first remove the excuse that the student is not sufficiently prepared.

I could easily imagine that for most students, their first college semester might start in June of their senior year of high school. They would have three months to pass the exams or get tutoring and small group instruction necessary to pass exams necessary to prove they were prepared for the maximum of four courses that they will be permitted to register for in September. (Remember our earlier chapter. Four courses in the fall. Four courses in the spring. Two or three courses the following summer.)

In addition, the first summer semester would be one where students take a course in study skills that include all of the topics covered in the first chapters in this book (and more).

September arrives. The students are admitted to Calculus I. The college is focused on seeing that at least 90% of the students aren't just passing, but master the course content.

In the first class, students are welcomed and assigned (as homework) to watch the first of what will eventually be 40 online video lectures. The video lecture will probably not be taught by the course instructor. Instead, the video will be from a selection of competing videos where the instructor selects the one most likely to result in success for their students.

Before the lecture begins, the student will be prompted for their ID. The video ID and the student ID will be stored in a national database whose purpose will become clear shortly.

In addition to the video, each student will be assigned homework that causes the student to apply their new knowledge. Then, there will be an online quiz. In schools where cheating is a concern, the test may be administered in a supervised (proctored) environment at the library or at a testing center set up for this purpose.

As a result of the post-lecture quiz, teachers will understand which lectures are effective and which are less so. An online catalogue of video lectures will always have noted the percent of students whose quiz grade reflects, mastery of the material.

How the word "mastery" is used in this book:

When I say "mastery," I mean the student has demonstrated
that they have integrated required material into their
capabilities such that the teacher and college is assured that
they have a solid foundation for the next task, class, section,
or advanced course.

I have intentionally not referred to letter grade or percentage
or a "curved" grade. Once we used nationally recognized
quizzes and exams, those tests should be neither too easy nor
too difficult. If they are too easy, then they will be quickly
identified as too many of those who pass will fail the next
course.
If they are too hard, then it will show as too many students
will fail the current course and the reputation of the teacher
and the college will publicly suffer (and deservedly so).

In addition, a small (single digit) percentage of students will be
given a competing lecture. Over time, this approach will enable
lectures that are more effective to rise.

The videos are selected by the teacher. The quizzes are
developed by national boards of teachers and the class teacher
should be able to select from quizzes whose track record
predicts success on the final exam.

If the students were all qualified to take the course and the
teacher able to select the best video and the best quiz, we are on
the right track to ensure student success.

Now consider a student that fails the quiz for lecture number
sixteen. (Again, arbitrary number.) For whatever reason, that
student may need personal tutoring or small group instruction or

it may just be that the student did not connect with that particular lecturer.

Over the last several decades, we have come to understand that different people respond to different types of teaching. In time, we may give students personality tests to understand which type of lectures or textbooks or other ways of receiving information works for them. However, in the beginning, comments by individuals who have seen the video lectures (similar to reviews on Amazon.com) may serve as a crude but effective tool to select alternate material when the first one does not resonate with an individual student.

Upon failing a quiz, the student's focus is not to "muscle through" and try to learn their material while simultaneously trying to keep up with additional material the class is absorbing. That approach would never be acceptable in the business world and should be eliminated from the college environment as well.

Instead, we declare a "mini-emergency" and a combination of tutoring, alternate lectures, and small group instruction should be given to the student until they pass the quiz. If the student takes a couple of days to do so that is ok. If there is one topic that the student takes three weeks to pass, that is OK as well. The point is that we do not accept anything less than topic mastery.

Depending on course experience, the teacher (or the math department) may schedule "slack" time in the schedule. This is a fundamental practice in Project Management where in this case we expect a certain number of students to fall behind and so while the semester may be scheduled for 16 weeks, that the syllabus schedules all work for 12. Students who are able to complete all quizzes and the final national exam in 12 weeks can finish the course early.

For the majority of those who learn at a slower pace, there is time to complete the course at their own pace.

"But wait," moans the teacher. "This means that in a classroom of 24 students, that by the middle of the semester, they will be scattered through the chapters!"

"Absolutely," I reply. "With lectures, exercises, and quizzes all assigned and presented outside of the classroom, time in the classroom can be spent by students helping each other in small groups, and teachers serving as consultants who move from group to group offering sage advice and probing questions where appropriate.

Now let's take a look at how the college, not just the teacher, helps during the semester. At a department or higher level, the progress of every student is tracked every week. From the moment a student fails a quiz, that student is emailed a mandatory invitation to immediately show up at the college's tutoring center to agree on a plan to master the topic content as quickly as possible.

This is no different than how in a professional environment, a STEM professional would meet with their supervisor to remediate a project that has fallen behind the schedule.

The plan might be as simple as agreeing to work with a tutor or small group or select an alternate video lecture or textbook. In any case, the student knows that whether in person or via conference call, that there will be a required daily check in from the day they fail a quiz until the day they finally pass the quiz.

This is where a college administration earns their salaries. Assume students are free to take their class anywhere, from any college, and are free to take the online national exams. At that point, a college tour will emphasize the steps the college takes when a student falls behind. Suddenly, student athletics, gourmet cafeteria food, and homecoming events may seem much less important to prospective students.

(On the other hand, if students are free to take less expensive and higher quality academic courses elsewhere, perhaps the college environment that includes luxurious dorms, spas, gyms, and athletic facilities that enable the student to also pursue their studies, will be precisely why a student will be willing to choose that college.)

Suppose a course includes 40 quizzes and by the end of the semester, the student has passed only 19 or 20. If by then end of the calendar semester, a student has passed less than half of the material, then it might be reasonable to assume that there is little chance they would complete the course over two semesters. Here we have a failure. However, if the student has mastered at least half the material, it is reasonable to assume that the trajectory for that student is to successfully complete the course, but at a slower pace.

In the case of a failure, a meeting with the student's college advisor takes place. Was the failure due to the student having personal issues? Was the student distracted and not have enough time to study? We already determined that the student had sufficient prerequisite knowledge, (via prerequisite exam,) had the best of national lectures, and had side tutoring and small group instruction to boot. Did we have a case where the instructor's command of the English language was so poor that this particular student could not understand explanations?

If the student attended most of the classes and at least attempted most of the homework, they should be given an opportunity to repeat the course AT NO COST the following semester with a different instructor. If they wish, they may always retake their course elsewhere if they are willing to pay. (With the removal of course transfer limitations, this should never be an issue.)

Based on this approach, there should be many fewer failures to deal with.

The Slow and Steady Student

Now consider the case of the student who masters 20 or more of the 40 required quizzes. We learn from Jean Piaget, the great child psychologist, that different people mature and learn at different rates. A student who has absolutely mastered the course content, but at a slower rate than their peers, should not be immediately failed. Instead, the student should be automatically admitted to the next semester Calculus I class without charge. In fact, with what were previously "Weeder" classes, some colleges may set up classes that are specifically for those students who take two semesters to master what in one semester was a Weeder course.

Course Quality

Much has been written in the popular press over the years about "grade inflation," especially in Liberal Arts and Business Programs [33] where the average GPA is around 3.3. [36] At the same time, despite recruiting students with high GPAs, SAT scores, class rankings, and math backgrounds, the GPAs of STEM students (especially, but not limited to Engineering and Science students) average a miserable 2.9 or less. [36]

This book proposes introducing some powerful market-based pressures that will penalize schools who fail to start delivering acceptable results. As a result of these pressures suggested in this text, there may be a temptation for colleges to reduce the high standards for their grading of courses as an improper shortcut to reducing failure rates.

One solution to prevent such abuse is to recognize that for most STEM courses that are already part of national standard curriculums, there should also be competing independent final exams. Just as the ACT and SAT exams compete as tests to rate student preparedness for college, so too should college teachers be recruited to develop national exams for Calculus I, II, and II, Organic Chemistry, Engineering Technology, and (almost) every other course within standardized curriculums.

It would be up to both colleges and their accreditation bodies to certify any given exam as acceptable.

Like Thomas Edison University TECEP, the national CLEP - College-Level Examination Program and DSST Exams (formerly DANTES), each forty-course bachelor's program requires a test that confirms subject mastery for probably 30 or 35 subjects. (Subjective courses such as Creative Writing, Acting, or Public Speaking would be exempt from such exams.)

I envision a system where these exams could be given by any participating college nationwide at any time for somewhere between $10 and $100 per exam attempt.

If a student passed the exam, their college would be required to accept the results for credit and not be allowed to charge more than a similar processing fee to accept the course.

By pursuing this path, a student would be free to pay the premium to attend a class in Chemistry at Lafayette, where the labs provide a terrific environment to internalize the tedious class work. Another student might take the same class online for a much less cost through Thomas Edison University. Still another might go to their local library every night after work or view YouTube videos and read Wikipedia articles prior to taking the exam.

The bottom line is that if individual classes were part of a free market for knowledge, then each student could choose the combination of classes within their budget and according to their educational needs.

Any school that refused to accept the results of the independent exams or refused to lower school costs for students who used these exams would not be eligible for their students to receive government-backed student loans.

(Note that is repeated throughout this text: In the future, those colleges limiting the number of outside credits that they would accept toward their diplomas should be required to disclose that for most majors, credits can be transferred to Excelsior College, Thomas Edison University, or Charter Oak University who award fully accredited diplomas. If there is a popular STEM major not offered by those colleges, then the government may fund their expansion.)

Schools would be expected and required to substitute the national exams for their own final exams for most of their courses. As a result, course quality will be maintained while competitive pressures may greatly lower the expense of certain courses for individual students based on their individual needs.

This approach would likely also pressure colleges to either dramatically slash the costs charged for "lecture hall" courses or eliminate them altogether. After all, if a student can pay the same course tuition at another college to sit in a class of 40 students, why would they pay the identical fee to sit in a lecture hall where the teacher's attention is divided between 400 (or more) students?

Chapters for Legislators and Regulators

These chapters are divided into two sections.

The first collection of chapters makes the case as to the "government interests" that justify government intervention in the ways that colleges operate.

The second collection of chapters propose specific actions whose intent is to increase the cost-effective delivery of qualified STEM graduates to the workforce.

Ralph Nader

Ralph Nader wrote a book at a time when people bought their cars based on style, comfort, and acceleration. By making people aware of safety issues, he changed consumer behavior and also legal and regulatory environments. In no small part due to Ralph Nader, today's cars are dramatically safer than they were decades ago. This book hopes to spark change in both consumer and legal environments as they apply to education so that people like me will no longer refer to our system of STEM education as a "scam."

An excerpt from Nader's Wikipedia entry:

Ralph Nader began to write about consumer safety issues in articles published in the Harvard Law Record, a student publication of Harvard Law School. He first criticized the automobile industry in 1959 in an article, "The Safe Car You Can't Buy", published by The Nation.

In 1965, Nader wrote the book Unsafe at Any Speed, in which he claimed that many American automobiles were unsafe to operate. The first chapter, "The Sporty Corvair - The One-Car Accident", pertained to the Corvair manufactured by the Chevrolet division of General Motors (GM), which had been involved in accidents involving spins and rollovers. More than 100 lawsuits were pending against GM related to accidents involving the popular compact car. Nader based his initial investigations into car safety on these lawsuits.

Nader's advocacy of automobile safety and the publicity

generated by the publication of Unsafe at Any Speed, along with concern over escalating nationwide traffic fatalities, contributed to Congress' unanimous passage of the 1966 National Traffic and Motor Vehicle Safety Act. The act established the National Highway Traffic Safety Administration, marking a historic shift in responsibility for automobile safety from the consumer to the government.

The legislation mandated a series of safety features for automobiles, beginning with safety belts and stronger windshields. The National Traffic and Motor Vehicle Safety Act was the first mandatory federal safety standards for motor vehicles. Speaker of the United States House of Representatives John William McCormack said the passage of the National Traffic and Motor Vehicle Safety Act was due to the "crusading spirit of one individual who believed he could do something...Ralph Nader." [69]

Ralph Nader brought automotive safety to the attention of both public and the government. That attention made clear that automotive safety regulation and safety test publication were areas that were appropriate for government action.

As a result of government actions, hundreds of thousands of deaths and millions of injuries have been prevented over the subsequent decades as government-mandated safety improvements (such as seatbelts and airbags) have been implemented across the industry.

In this chapter, I explain the "government interest" in reducing the number of STEM failures.

I also explain the small number of laws and regulations that can have a positive impact on reducing the number of STEM student failures the current system produces each year while also providing incentives for colleges to better control their costs.

Government Interest

My libertarian-leaning friends feel the problems of American colleges will only be made worse by increasing government intervention. Eliminate government funding and regulations and the market will take care of itself, they say.

While I respectfully disagree, I understand their reservations considering the consequences in many areas when the government does overreach. As a result, I will do my best to offer suggestions that I see as the minimum required to induce colleges to improve the quality of their services.

I submit that there are multiple reasons why it will be proper, prudent, and reasonable for the government to take certain steps to increase market forces and other motivations that will cause colleges to take steps to increase the number of qualified and competent graduates of STEM majors provided to the U.S. economy.

There are multiple areas negatively impacted by the existing system. They include:
- Economic Contributions by STEM Graduates
- US Company Motivation Keeps STEM Jobs Offshore
- US Economy Competitive Position
- Household Formation
- Marriage and Reproduction Impact
- Housing Market Values

- Construction Industry Impact
- Student Loan Default Rates
- US Credit Market Impact
- Impact on Income Tax Revenues
- Impact on U.S. Health Care Costs
- Impact on U.S. Business Formation
- The Government as Student Loan Borrower

Economic Contributions by STEM Graduates

Companies generally hire and pay people relative to the value they add to the company's bottom line. The reason STEM graduates are generally paid more than other college, trade school, and high school graduates, is that their services as scientists, engineers, and physicians create the software, hardware, medications, media, and other contributions that keep the U.S. economy growing.

By failing to educate forty to sixty percent of those students who enter STEM programs, the economy is deprived of the services those students would be creating as graduates.

The lost wages of the failed STEM student cohort represent a negative impact on U.S. Gross Domestic Product. With an average annual graduation of more than 350,000 STEM students, we can roughly estimate that another 350,000 either fail out of college or switch to a less-lucrative liberal arts or business career. Considering the lifetime loss of wages, [107] we can roughly estimate that an additional 350 billion dollars in future wages are lost every year due to these unnecessary failures.

Company Motivation Keeps Jobs Offshore

There has been much written about the offshore relocation of relatively low-paying manufacturing jobs. But there has also been some press about why the shortage of STEM workers is part of the reason companies like Apple needs to keep much of their manufacturing in China and Germany. Consider this passage from Steve Jobs biography:

Apple had 700,000 factory workers employed in China, (Jobs) said, and that was because it needed 30,000 engineers on-site to support those workers. "You can't find that many in America to hire," he said. These factory engineers did not have to be PhDs or geniuses; they simply needed to have basic engineering skills for manufacturing. Tech schools, community colleges, or trade schools could train them. "If you could educate these engineers," he said, "we could move more manufacturing plants here." (Steve Jobs, p. 546).

This and Tim Cook quotes at http://www.huffingtonpost.com/2012/12/06/apple-manufacturing-usa-macs_n_2249613.html.
(119)

As a result of the limited availability of STEM graduates, U.S. companies will continue to be motivated to locate facilities in China, Sweden, Germany, and other countries producing and hiring STEM educated people.

Again, we have a further negative impact on the U.S. G.D.P.

US Economy Competitive Position

In the 1800s, the U.S. economy (and those of other developed nations) slowly transformed from agriculture based on property to manufacturing based on materials.

In the 1900s the U.S. economy (and those of other developed nations) transformed increasingly from manufacturing to technology and then to knowledge-based services.

In the 21st century, the ability of the U.S. economy to provide well-paying jobs to the workforce increasingly depends on the ability to educate the workforce in areas needed for U.S. companies to operate in a globally competitive environment.

Every STEM student who fails out of school subtracts from the pool of knowledgeable resources available to maintain national competitive capabilities.

In addition, the success of other countries in ramping up the production of STEM degree granting institutions should motivate the U.S. to improve our labor pool of these competitive resources. According to the Organisation for Economic Cooperation and Development (OECD), China and India combined currently represents about 29% of college graduates. This number is projected to increase to 41% of all college graduates by 2020, only a few years from now. [91]

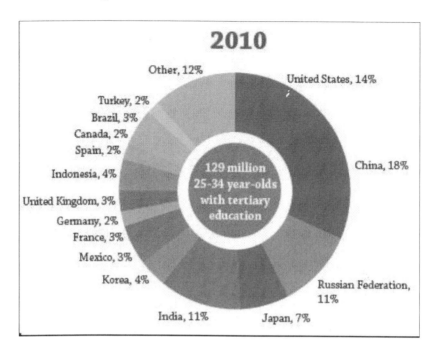

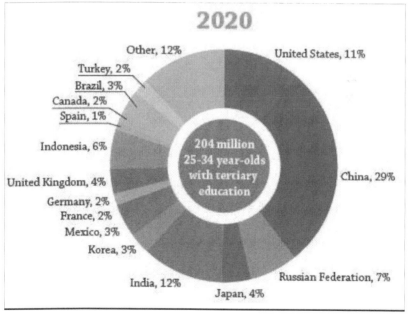

Both Charts [91]

Household Formation

As reported by the Pew Research Center and National Public Radio, 29% of women and 35% of men between the ages of 18 and 34 are currently living at home. [14] [120] This is the highest percentage since the 1940's during the tail end of the Great Depression.

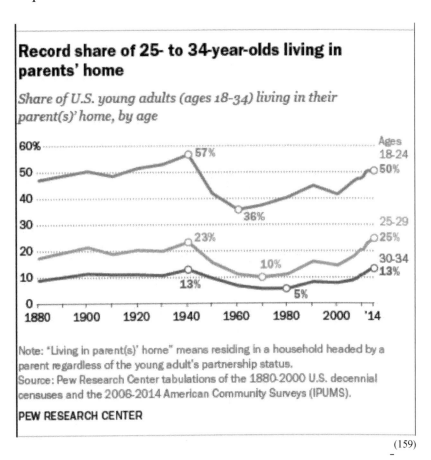

Record share of 25- to 34-year-olds living in parents' home

Share of U.S. young adults (ages 18-34) living in their parent(s)' home, by age

Note: "Living in parent(s)' home" means residing in a household headed by a parent regardless of the young adult's partnership status.
Source: Pew Research Center tabulations of the 1880-2000 U.S. decennial censuses and the 2006-2014 American Community Surveys (IPUMS).

PEW RESEARCH CENTER

(159)

One reason women are doing better than men in terms of moving out is that while the percentage of men who graduate from college has been flat over the last fifteen years, the percentage of women who graduate from college now exceeds the percentage of men.

While some professions (such as nurses) have traditionally been dominated by women, other professions (such as engineers) have been dominated by men.

If we reduce the number of STEM failures, we may increase the numbers of individuals able to leave home and form new households. There are multiple impacts on the economy, on society, and on the government if we achieve these goals.

College attainment by gender

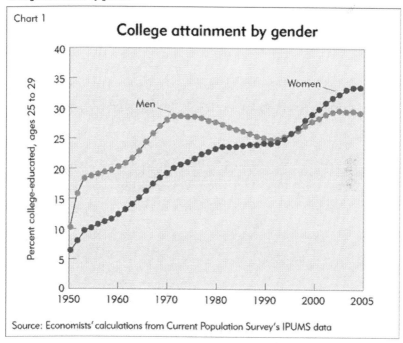

Pew Research Chart [120]

The Consumer Reports Survey (CRS)

(133)

In March-April, 2016 the Consumer Reports National Research Center conducted a nationally representative online survey to assess the availability and usefulness of high school and college financial aid guidance and student loan debt and its impact on financial, lifestyle and relationship choices. GfK Group administered the survey to a nationally representative sample of 1,550 adult U.S. residents from March 31 - April 9, 2016. The sample is 53% female with an average age of 29. To qualify for the survey, a panel member must have: 1. been between 21 and 40 years old; and 2. had student loan debt. (133)

In various passages that follow, statements credited to CRS (133) are quoted from that report.

According to the CRS survey, 28% of respondents reported that they "Had to live with my parents/other family members longer than I wanted." (131)

Marriage and Reproduction Impact

Household formation is directly correlated with marriage and reproduction.

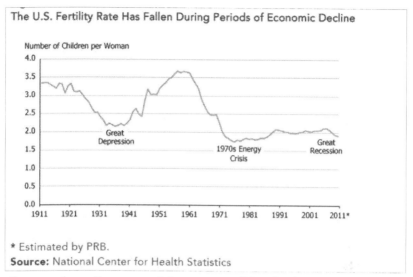

Source: http://www.socialmatter.net/2014/12/23/reproduction-and-its-substitute/ [160]

As shown by the chart above, the U.S. fertility rate has dropped in each of the last three periods of economic decline.

Fertility is important as replacing population is essential to put in place the next generation of taxpayers to support social programs and a growing economy.

Taking steps to decrease STEM failure rates and subsequently INCREASE the number of people studying STEM subjects would likely address a portion of this issue.

According to the CRS Survey, 12% of respondents "Experienced a strained or failed relationship because of student loan debt." [131] In addition, 12% reported that delayed getting married due to their debt.

Housing Market Values

Like any other product, housing values are maintained (or increased) when demand exceeds supply. While not every failed STEM student represents a decrease in future home purchases, they are a factor.

In the CRS survey, 28% of respondents answered that they "Delayed buying a house" because of their student debt. [131]

Construction Industry Impact

The Great Recession headlines focused on an overheated housing market fueled from the bottom by the sub-prime market. However, missing from those headlines were the flattening of college graduation, especially, but not limited to, males.

Decrease the number of STEM student failures and we increase the demand for entry-level housing and related construction.

Student Loan Default Rates

As reported by the Federal Reserve to USA Today in 2015, [15] only four percent of individuals with bachelor's degrees were behind on payments on their student loans. At the same time, "21% of those who have no degree and are no longer enrolled in the program for which they borrowed" were behind on payments.

US Credit Market Impact

As shown in the diagram below, the percentage of U.S. consumer debt composed of student loans has grown to 10% of the total. Unlike mortgage debt which is secured by real estate properties, the student debt is only as good as the students' ability to repay the debt.

Taking actions to lower failure rates would over time, reduce outstanding loan balances and the drag those balances represent on the credit market and the economy.

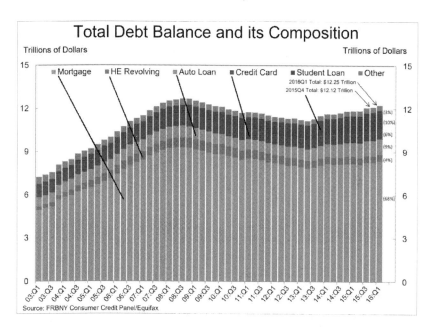

https://www.newyorkfed.org/medialibrary/interactives/househol
dcredit/data/pdf/HHDC_2016Q1.pdf   (16)

Income Tax Revenue Impact

STEM graduates make dramatically more money than STEM failures and pay dramatically more income taxes as a result.

America's colleges currently graduate about 350,000 of their STEM students each year. (93)

Lifetime earnings from STEM students is approximately $3.5 million dollars. (95)

FIGURE 1: MEDIAN LIFETIME EARNINGS BY HIGHEST EDUCATIONAL ATTAINMENT, 2009 DOLLARS

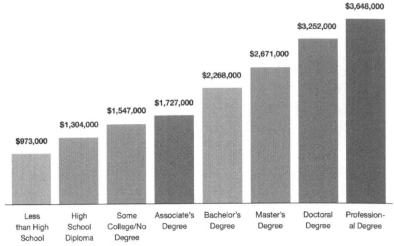

(95)

Some of those STEM students will change majors, obtain a bachelor's degree, and then go on to other careers. Some will drop out of college, convinced that they are not "college material."

The chart above reflects the income for ALL professions, including STEM. On average, lifetime earnings for those with some college but not a degree are $1.5 million dollars. Those with a Bachelor's on average earn $2.2 million dollars. (Of those with Bachelor's degrees, those who majored in STEM subjects generally earn more than those who majored in other areas.)

Those with a STEM degree (from the previous chart) average $3.5 million dollars.

Imagine if each year, we could save 80% of the 350,000 students who would otherwise fail out of STEM programs each year. The average additional lifetime earnings for each of the 280,000 additional graduates would be in excess of one million dollars. The total lifetime loss of income (and by extension, lost to the economy) would be $2.8 billion dollars.

Add another $2.8 billion dollars in lost future earnings each year we keep failing the majority of those students.

It actually gets worse as the number of students enrolled in STEM programs has risen every year for the last decade. [93]

The total lost income over the next twenty years calculates to about $60 billion dollars. That is $60 billion dollars lost to the economy and $20 or more billion dollars in lost tax revenues.

US Health Care Cost Impact

The vast majority of STEM graduates (and their families) are able to either gain employment that includes employer-provided health care or gain professional income where they can afford healthcare without government subsidy. However, a portion of the STEM failures requires subsidies for their health care due to their lower overall income.

US Business Formation Impact

A portion of STEM graduates go on to become entrepreneurs or work for new businesses. Each STEM student failure represents a lessening of the resources available to start and/or work for these new businesses.

The Government as Student Loan Borrower

The majority of student loans are not just the responsibility of students and their families, they are the responsibility of the federal government who guarantees most of those loans. If the government is on the hook for the tab, there should be some conditions of accountability by the colleges that they are providing a service that is both cost-effective and of quality for those funds.

Projected Reversal of Immigration Trends

In 2012, President Obama accepted the recommendations of the President's Council of Advisors on Science and Technology (PCAST), whose *Engage to Excel* report called for producing "one million additional college graduates with bachelor or associate degrees in STEM fields" over the next decade." [96]

Since then, the number of students enrolled in such programs has steadily risen. [93]

However, some globalization trends may mean that the U.S. may be faced with a shortage despite these efforts. This is due in large part to economic successes in India and China, (two countries that have long supplied the U.S. with STEM-educated professionals). [93]

India Considerations

In my various technology executive roles, I hired and worked with many people from India (and surrounding countries including Pakistan). The services of these individuals have contributed to the US's Gross National Product. Some claim that by increasing the supply of imported labor, the supply-demand equation had led to lower wages, especially for Information Technology professionals. To an extent, I accept this is basic economics and is true.

However, I have also observed that for Information Technology (IT) professionals who have kept their skills current, that there is no shortage of jobs in the $70,000 to $120,000 compensation range. Therefore, the impact of the Indian professionals has not impoverished anyone who accepts continuing skill acquisition as a requirement of a technology career.

On the positive side, the supply of Information Technology professionals has enabled startups and established companies who can afford to pay such wages to hire both U.S. citizens and foreigners instead of offshoring all of their development.

If we were to lose these professionals, companies would not, as is claimed by some, increase wages and train up U.S. citizens. My experience is that at a critical point, the vast majority of the remaining IT jobs would be outsourced to other countries.

I can only conclude that the net impact of the foreigners is to protect and increase the net demand for the highest-level U.S. based workers.

In the case of individuals from India, however, the current equation appears to be changing.

As reported by Dina Bass at Bloomberg News in 2015, Indian STEM graduates from American colleges are increasingly making the decision to return home to pursue jobs in their rapidly growing economies. [87]

> Ms. Bass recounts the experience of Kunal Bahl. Mr. Bass, armed with Ivy League degrees in business and engineering, worked at Microsoft Corporation. His U.S. visa was rejected and he was deported home to India. Once in India, he founded Snapdeal. "Today Snapdeal.com is one of the most highly valued startups in Asia's third-largest economy, valued

at about $5 billion." Today, "many Indians aren't leaving at all, or are going to the U.S. for degrees from Harvard and Stanford with no plans to stay after graduation." [87] [And this was written prior to the election of 2016!]

According to the article, "Venture capitalists and hedge funds are swooping in with aims to profit on startups like Snapdeal. Venture financing in Indian tech companies hit $1.9 billion in the fourth quarter, almost six times the $325 million in the year-earlier period, according to CB Insights. Snapdeal alone landed $627 million from SoftBank Corp. (The company has had several rounds of funding, and the last, which made Japan's SoftBank its largest investor, valued it at $5 billion, Bahl says.)" [87]

Hedge funds, investment firms and asset managers have pumped $3.8 billion into 26 Indian tech startups since the beginning of last year, according to data compiled by Bengaluru-based Tracxn. [87]

According to the article, six Indian tech startups are already valued at $1 billion or more. This represents thousands and thousands of jobs which will never materialize in the U.S. More from the article:

> It's not just startups employing engineers and others in India; Apple Inc., Amazon.com Inc., Microsoft and other U.S. tech giants have offices across the country. [87]

As India increases its attractiveness to U.S. graduates, the U.S. will need to graduate more of its own citizens. One way to do that is to continue the same practices as we do today. Of course, an easier and less costly approach is to reduce the number of students who fail due to deficiencies in today's system.

China Considerations

Like India, China has long been a source for STEM expertise for American businesses. Also like India, China is starting to attract its citizens back from the U.S. to work with its fast-growing economy.

The following text is drawn from the book, *Reverse Migration in Contemporary China: Returnees, Entrepreneurship and the Chinese Economy (Politics and Development of Contemporary China)* Kindle Edition, by Huiyao Wang and Yue Bao. (https://www.amazon.com/Reverse-Migration-Contemporary-China-Entrepreneurship-ebook/dp/B0161IX6V4/ref=dp_kinw_strp_1/178-0082900-4558945).

(88)

In today's technology-focused world economy, there is a "global brain circulation" and a "global talent war." In most of the last four decades, educated technology and medical professionals had routinely migrated from "developing" or "emerging" countries to the developed wealthier countries of the world.

Ever since the start of the 2008 Global Economic Crisis, large numbers of these professionals have returned to their home countries. To maintain and accelerate this trend, China policy makers have encouraged the attraction of venture capital to help transform the economy "from manufacturing to a knowledge-based economy."

Much of that venture capital will fund salaries for technology and healthcare workers.

As of 2013, China had sent 3.05 million students to study

abroad and 818,400 had already returned home. China sees those who have not yet returned home as "significant potential source for expanding China's small pool of innovative and high-tech talent."

"In 2010, the CPC Central Committee and Chinese government State Council jointly issued the nation Medium and Long Term Talent Development Plan (2010 – 2020) establishing a blueprint for creating a highly skilled national workforce within the next 10 years. … Among the plan's goals in the transformation of China from a manufacturing center to a world innovation hub, a grand objective that will be met in part by increasing its talent pool from the current 114 million people to 180 million people by 2020."

"Since 1995, the number of returnees has gone up by 13 percent annually."

"In 2011, some 186,000 individuals returned to China, a nearly threefold increase compared with 2008."

"These returnees were highly educated, with advanced degrees in management, technology, or science. Some 51 percent of them held master's degrees and 41 percent had PhDs. The combination of homegrown talent with those returning from abroad has improved the education, skills, and creativity of the Chinese workforce."

(88)

Combine the impact of India with impact of China and America's competitive position in the high tech and medical professions may eventually be at risk!

Colleges are failing from 40% to 60% of their STEM customers.

We wouldn't put up with that kind of a failure rate from our automobile manufacturers and we sure as hell should not put up with that kind of failure rate from our colleges.

Chapters for Legislator & Regulator Actions

The Roadmap
In the previous chapter, I laid out why the government has an interest in both reducing the number of students who fail out of STEM programs and at the same time, increase the number of qualified STEM graduates who enter the workforce. This chapter advocates those actions the government should consider accomplishing in pursuit of those goals.

Strategies
There are a very few and limited actions (tactics) that the government can take to improve the number of students who successfully graduate with accredited STEM degrees, to lower the cost of those degrees, and lower the loan default rates and other negative impacts of the current situation.

Those actions will support the following three strategies:
1. Enable students to make more informed purchasing decisions.
2. Motivate colleges to operate more efficiently.
3. Motivate colleges to improve outcomes.

Tactics
The proposed tactics that support the above strategies are:
1. Independent exam development.
2. Loans for courses, not programs.
3. Develop & publicize college and course ranking metrics relevant to educational success.
4. Tie student loan borrowing limits to expected outcomes.
5. Implement incentives that favor schools that do not limit the inbound transfer of credits.
6. Legislate advisor fiduciary responsibility.
7. Increasing teacher quality.

The details, pros, and cons, of each of these tactics are explained below.

1. Independent Exam Development

In order to measure course and teacher quality, encourage the development of independent final exams for the majority of required courses by requiring use of such tests to qualify for loans.

As noted elsewhere in the book, there are more than 100 exams already on the market for various courses that are accepted by fully accredited colleges. By requiring the development of these exams for the vast majority of STEM courses, we will have an independent resource to determine if students are mastering the course material or whether teachers are inflating grades in order to earn performance bonuses.

As suggested in the prior text, these exams might be developed by committees of teachers in cooperation with the existing accreditation bodies.

Colleges should be given a year to set up committees and a year to implement the exams. After that, a portion of college loans could be "held back" until the exams were implemented.

2. Loans for courses, not programs

It is time to make loans for college courses, not semesters. (Room and board would be a separate loan.) By requiring reporting of final results and teacher IDs, policies could eventually be adopted to discourage borrowers from "purchasing" courses from incompetent teachers. (Course

tuition would be required to include ALL related expenses
including textbooks, lab fees, technology fees, etc.)

The suggestion here borrows the lesson the country learned
when trying to improve performance of our nation's hospitals.
For many years, certain hospitals seemed to have very high total
Medicare insurance reimbursements because too many patients
were quickly discharged and then quickly readmitted for the
same or worsening conditions. That second admission resulted
in the hospital being paid twice to treat the same condition.

The problem here was that many of the patients could have been
completely cured with a slightly longer initial stay. Other
patients could have avoided the need for readmission by some
home visits by nurses, physical therapists, and others to ensure
that patients took their medications and healed properly at
home.

After years of minimal progress at reducing readmissions,
Medicare administrators started to financially penalize hospitals
with excessive admission rates.

In 2012, more than 2,000 hospitals were penalized. By 2014,
the program was in full effect and 2,610 hospitals were
penalized. By 2015, changes in hospital polices started to
take effect and the number of penalized hospitals fell to
2,592.

(100) (101) (102)

As shown in the following chart, there is still a wide variation
between readmission rates between hospitals with a similar mix
of patients:

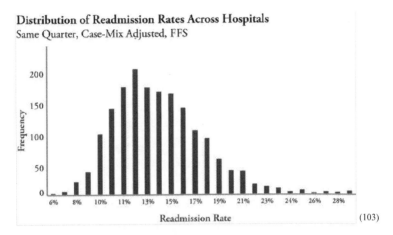

Distribution of Readmission Rates Across Hospitals
Same Quarter, Case-Mix Adjusted, FFS

(103)

During this time, despite reluctance from many doctors and hospitals to take actions that reduce their income, overall progress has been slow but steady.

"After staying constant in the 19-19.5% range from 2007-2011, the all-cause 30-day readmission rate for Medicare Patients dropped to 18.5% in 2012 and dropped further to 17.5% in 2013. All told, CMS estimates that this decline translates into an estimated 150,000 avoided hospital readmissions." (105)

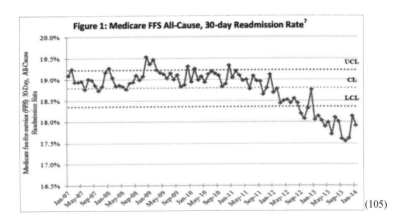

(105)

So, this government action to make hospitals be more accountable for their actions has reduced readmissions by more than 150,000. This not only saved taxpayers a lot of money, but reduced pain, suffering, and unnecessary early deaths.

In addition to being inspired by the success of the Medicaid program to improve hospital outcomes, we can also be inspired and learn from the original major consumer protection act.

In the last decade, we have come to realize that making home loans to people who could not afford to repay them is bad business. Looking back, one of the factors that caused the Great Recession was "sub-prime lending." Fortunately, we have now put into place laws and regulations intended to lessen the chances of a similar disaster. However, we have a similar issue in that we typically make college loans regardless of major.

Educated people have higher wages and lower unemployment rates than the less educated so why are college students at Occupy Wall Street protests around the country demanding forgiveness for crushing student debt? The sluggish economy is tough on everyone, but the students are also learning a hard lesson, going to college is not enough. You also have to study the right subjects. And American students are not studying the fields with the greatest economic potential.

Over the past 25 years, the total number of students in college has increased by about 50 percent. But the number of students graduating with degrees in science, technology, engineering and math (the so-called STEM fields) has remained more or less constant. Moreover, many of today's STEM graduates are foreign born and are taking their knowledge and skills back to their native countries.

Test from the website, *marginalrevolution.com*, **College has been oversold,** *by* Alex Tabarrok [92]

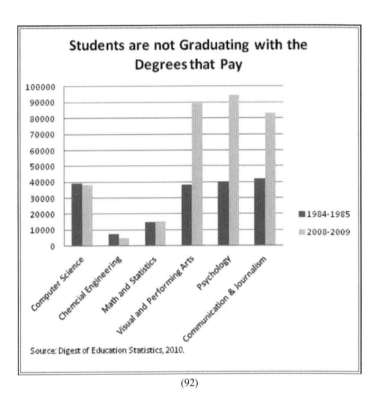

(92)

Considering the high incidence of non-STEM graduates who find themselves in low-paying jobs, it may be time to limit funding in those majors where there seems to be little prospect of debt repayment.

In those cases, the first two years of low-cost community college followed by the lowest possible cost state colleges may be a much better way to serve these students.

> While the majority of the suggestions in this book have to do
> with lowering net college costs and reforming or terminating
> incompetent institutions, I believe substantial increases of
> long-term government expenditures for community and state
> colleges are essential for U.S. economic health.
>
> It makes no sense to send a student to their local community
> college only to have them be told that they can only take a
> course or two as budget limitations mean the other needed
> courses are fully booked.

Legislating a Collegiate Lemon Law

The general quality of automobiles (both domestic and
international brands) has relentlessly improved over the years.
Notice I used the word "generally."

Once in a while, a truly awful car will roll off the production
line. Such a car's defects are not obvious until the car has been
sold and the new car buyer has had it for a few months.

Imagine if you are a typical new car buyer. In the United States,
automotive expenses are often the buyer's largest lifetime
expense after housing. While Uber and Zipcar are reducing the
reason to own a car, for millions of people, cars are a huge and
still necessary expense.

For many, cars are not only an expense, but a necessity. Many
people buy new cars because the purchase of a used car
increases the risk of days in the shop being repaired. For many
employers, employees who have regular transportation issues
are perceived as unreliable people and unreliable people need to
be replaced.

Now imagine you had the unfortunate luck to buy such a car. First, your transmission started making grinding noises so you returned the car to the dealer for repairs.

After a week, the dealer returned the car to you. Three weeks later, the transmission failed on your way to work.

After four such repeat trips to the dealer, your car's electrical system failed one morning.

Over a period of months, one thing after another kept failing. You lost days of work. Your employer became increasingly irritated and your job was at risk. At a certain point, it became clear to you that even if 99.6% of this model car sold to others were of high quality, that the car you had purchased was truly a piece of crap.

Now you return to the dealer and meet with the owner. You point out how patient you have been. You note the amount of salary you lost due to lateness at work, and that your employer is on the verge of firing you. Because of these realities, you either want your money back, or you want the dealer to take back your car in exchange for one that would not break.

The dealer was sympathetic to your situation, but not helpful. The best the dealer could do was continue to try to fix the car. After all, maybe you are being too rough on the car. Maybe you are driving over too many potholes. You don't think so, but the dealer knows that he sold this model of car to thousands of other buyers and none of those cars had a problem.

The vehicle manufacturer was equally unhelpful. In fact, once your warranty ran out, the dealer and manufacturer then charged you for the continuing repairs for your car that never worked as expected.

This used to be the actual relationship of American car dealers and manufacturers to the people who bought their cars. In the 1970s and 1980s, the number of people who experienced this adventure ran into the thousands and thousands each year.

The libertarian leaning conservative politicians wanted nothing to do with this. "After all," they reasoned, "if enough consumers had bad experiences, then the free market would eventually reduce sales and the manufacturers would eventually stop selling so many crap cars."

Year after year, the situation worsened. Occasionally, a wealthy car buyer would sue a manufacturer, but they were rarely a match for the massive legal teams of the manufacturers.

Liberal politicians started paying attention. Hearings were held. Consumer groups testified. The manufacturers also testified and warned against government interference with their businesses.
(134)

In the end, Congress passed a revolutionary piece of legislation called the "Lemon Law." Combined with other regulations, every consumer can now demand that after a certain number of major repairs in a specified time period, that the manufacturer now either refund the buyer's money or exchange the "Lemon" for a new car.

From Wikipedia: " **Lemon laws** are American state laws that provide a remedy for purchasers of cars and other consumer goods in order to compensate for products that repeatedly fail to meet standards of quality and performance. Although there may be defective products of all sorts ranging from small

electrical appliances to huge pieces of machinery, the term "lemon" is generally thought of as applying to defective vehicles such as automobiles, trucks, SUVs, and motorcycles. These vehicles and other goods are called "lemons". The federal lemon law (the Magnuson-Moss Warranty Act) was enacted in 1975 and protects citizens of all states. State lemon laws vary by state and may not necessarily cover used or leased cars, and other goods. The rights afforded to consumers by lemon laws may exceed the warranties expressed in purchase contracts. *Lemon law* is the common nickname for these laws, but each state has different names for the laws and acts."
(https://en.wikipedia.org/wiki/Lemon_law 5/9/2016) [134]

Not only that, but subsequent government regulations have led to manufacturers now tracking and disclosing repair and related defect statistics that the government, consumer groups, and individual attorneys use to keep automobile manufacturers accountable for the products they sell.

Not only did this finally achieve a small measure of justice for the car buyer, but incented the manufacturers to increase the quality of their product so they would not have the expense of so many refunds.

Some might argue that the Lemon Law is one of the motivating factors for the continuing quality improvements that has been the case with automobile manufacturers worldwide since the 1980's. (Yes, competition from the Japanese helped, but so did the Lemon Law.)

I believe the time has come to pass a College Lemon Law for certain, if not most, college courses.

The Interest of the US. Government

Such a law would recognize that as the U.S. government provides financing for millions of college students, and that provision of defective courses can lead to reduced incomes that jeopardize the ability of many students to repay their loans. This recognizes that in fact the U.S. government is a party to the financial transaction that purchases each College course.

Even if a student is not using a government backed loan to pay for college, the automotive Lemon Law provides precedent for a successful law that defended the rights of consumers without overreaching and negatively impacting the industry it targeted.

College Lemon Law Legal Basis

It all starts with the Uniform Commercial Code (UCC). The UCC is a set of laws adopted in similar forms by all U.S. states and territories. As explained in Wikipedia, the UCC has "with the goal of harmonizing the law of sales and other commercial transactions across the United States of America" [151]

Within the UCC is the concept of an "Implied Warranty," "the concept of product or service quality assurance or fitness for a specific purpose."

> As explained by the Cornell University Law School Online Legal Dictionary, "Where the seller at the time of contracting has reason to know any particular purpose for which the goods [or services] are required and that the buyer is relying on the seller's skill or judgment to select or furnish suitable goods, there is unless excluded or

modified under the next section an implied warranty that the goods shall be fit for such purpose."

In the case of college courses and programs, the seller is a college which is a multi-million-dollar enterprise employing lawyers, marketers, and subject matter experts in the course material. The purchasers are often minors or other individuals who must rely on the representations of the schools as to the suitability of the courses for the purchaser.

For a college to take the student's money for a course without ascertaining the likelihood of the students' chances of successfully completing the course when the college has a history of a large percentage of students failing that course amounts (in my layperson's opinion) to fraud.

Defining STEM Lemon Law Covered Courses

For most STEM courses, the final grade shall be based on an exam independent of the college, but accepted as authoritative by both the college and one of the regional accreditation bodies previously discussed.

As an example, let's consider Calculus I. This is a course required of many STEM majors and often taken during the freshman year.

Successful mastery of Calculus I is important for multiple reasons. First, a student who only achieves partial mastery of Calculus I is highly likely to fail Calculus II and any other future course where Calculus I skills are a prerequisite. Second, a low or failing grade jeopardizes the student's Grade Point Average which in turn threatens any financial aid. Third, a low or failing grade can demoralize a student and eventually contribute to the student withdrawing from the STEM program if not college altogether.

For all of these reasons, let us agree that mastery of Calculus I is critical to the success of a particular STEM major and one that an independent exam can effectively and efficiently judge whether the student has mastered the course material.

We should start by ascertaining whether a student is qualified to take this particular course. Traditionally, colleges have used a combination of high school transcripts and either SAT or ACT scores to qualify students for this course. However, the high failure rate experienced by students in Calculus I combined with the high failure rate of such students in Calculus II indicates that many students may not be sufficiently prepared to take this course.

As a result, no college shall permit any student to register for Calculus I until they have passed an independent exam that ensures they are qualified.

The exam shall be developed and administered by an independent organization recognized by both the college and their regional accrediting body. Just as the SAT and ACT producers compete for acceptance by colleges, there may be any number of Calculus I exams competing for use by the colleges.

The math department of the college should decide which independent test measuring course preparedness shall be administered. After all, in the coming world where they will be held accountable for results, unqualified students should be diverted into remedial classes until they truly have the required background.

Every student who takes such a qualification exam shall later take a post course final exam. The teacher of the course shall also be noted.

The college may determine what constitutes a passing grade for the qualification test or may defer to the national body they selected the test from. If, for example, experience shows that a student who passes a high school math test (for trigonometry, algebra, and geometry) with a 95% score has a 95% probability of earning an A or B in Calculus, then the college may require such a score on such an exam to earn the right to register for calculus in their college.

For any given course, the college shall report to a national database the following within 15 days of the start of the course

- College name and ID number
- Teacher name and ID number
- Course name and ID number
- Course scheduled start date and scheduled completion date
- Student ID number
- Pre-qualification test ID
- Student's Pre-qualification test score

By reporting these items at the outset, there can later be visibility and accountability with regard to the results.

At any time during the course, the student may go online and take "practice" post-course exams which shall be just as difficult and comprehensive as the final post-course "Certification" exam.

During the last two weeks of the exam, the student will take a "Proctored" "Final" exam supervised by an employee of the college who did not teach any part of this course to this student.

The student may take the Final exam up to once a week for the following four weeks if the student feels they would like to try to improve their final grade.

The testing organization will report or update only the highest final grade achieved by the student.

The final results of this process will be available in real time on a web accessible database.

- By reporting the percentage of students whose score indicates subject mastery, a determination can be made as to whether the pre-qualification test was sufficiently rigorous.

- By continued reporting of the percentage of students who mastered the material by teacher, teachers can be rated and improved or replaced depending on the individual circumstance.

- Students whose grade indicates subject mastery shall be entitled to transfer this course to any other college who admits them. Any limitations on the number of courses eligible for transfer will be waived in the case of a student who, via the independent test, has demonstrated mastery of the subject. Yes, this will reduce some revenue for some colleges. But the net impact of this program will be to increase tuition revenue as more students succeed over their four-year adventure.

- Classes with less than 95% passing will be considered a teaching failure. All failing students will be eligible at no charge to take the course again, with a different teacher, and with nightly study groups supervised by a qualified tutor.

- Students who fail when 95% of the class passes will be considered to either be insufficiently prepared or for some reason unable to focus on their studies. Their following semester will be limited to either taking a remedial prerequisite course or retaking this course and at most one other course. They will be required to participate in small group tutoring at least four nights per week. Their tuition for that semester will be limited to only the two courses and no other academic fees of any kind. As different people have different learning styles, they will be offered a different teacher who shall have competent teaching and communication skills.

- No college shall require any student to take a course offered by a specific teacher. If no other teacher acceptable to the student is available, the student may take the course elsewhere and then transfer the results once achieving subject mastery as measured by independent examination. The historic, but never achieved, accountability goals of websites like RateMyProfessor.com will finally be achieved.

- Any student who attends 90% of both classes and tutoring sessions in the second semester and who fails a second time shall be given a full refund of their tuition. This is the "hammer" of accountability, which will require colleges to either negotiate accountability in their employment contracts with teachers or face bankruptcy. If automobile companies had a 5% failure rate of the cars they sold, they too would rightly be driven out of business.

There are some teachers who will react to this by saying "this is like letting the inmates run the asylum." They are entitled to their perception. To them, I reply, "No, this recognizes that you, as teachers, are providing a service to students who are your customers and who will now be able to steer where their funds are spent. They are your customers, and in a capitalist economy, the customer shall be king!"

Exceptions

To every rule and every system, there are exceptions. How to standardize a test for a creative writing course? I wouldn't try and we shouldn't try. However, in the vast majority of STEM courses, standardization of material happened years ago.

What about new material?

I would suggest that the independent organizations who develop the exams be required to contract with college teachers to develop the courses and then to keep the questions updated. As this approach encourages the development of competing tests (as with the SAT and the ACT). I could see committees of teachers from multiple colleges developing competing tests. However, such tests would have to be accepted by both college administrators and the relevant regional accrediting body.

Rather than focus only on teaching and research, colleges should reward teachers who contribute to committees that continually improve tests that should cover most courses within every STEM program.

Program Implementation Mechanics

I propose we learn from this success to hold colleges accountable for their services as well.

Let's consider what students borrow money for to pay for their education.

In most cases, student loans may be used to pay for separate fees including:

- Course tuition (May be a lump sum or may be by credit)
- Room (dormitory housing)
- Board (typically a meal plan)
- Books
- "Technology Support Surcharge"
- Computer and/or printer
- Student activity surcharge(s)
- Enrollment fees (per semester or per credit)
- Campus transportation surcharge
- Class supplies other than books for items such as lab or art materials
- Dormitory extras such as reading lamps, microwave, refrigerators, sheets, towels, cleaning service, laundry service, etc.
- Clothing and mobile phone
- Healthcare
- Application Fee
- Graduation and diploma fees
- Surcharges for athletic participation and/or athletic insurance
- Fraternity or Sorority and/or other club expenses
- Special library or other learning material access fee

Many colleges require students to live on campus. [48] All of this serves to confuse those families budgeting for college.

As noted previously, it takes between five and six years for the vast majority of STEM students to earn their bachelor's degrees, (with less than nine percent completing their degree in four years).

In this text, I have advocated that STEM student families plan for a six-year bachelor's adventure.

I suggest that we take the total of all college costs for six years and divide that number by the 40 courses each student must master in order to obtain their bachelor's degree.

That should be the tuition each student is charged. If the student does not live on campus, then the board and/or room fees are deducted.

For a college that traditionally costs $20,000 per year (of which $8,000 is room and board), the per course cost over six years would be $2,400 per course.

For a college that cost $65,000 per year (I'm looking at you, Drexel), the cost would be closer to $6,900 per course.

If a student graduates in four or five years instead of six, then the college could refund the savings to the student who would also start their career and start earning money and paying taxes that much sooner.

Student loans would be granted "provisionally." At the time the student registers for the class, the teacher, course, and college would all be noted in a national database. At the conclusion of the course, the college would receive a bonus or be fined a penalty depending on how the overall class performed in the post-course Independent Course Mastery Exam. (For details, refer to bonuses and penalties suggested to be paid to teachers later in the text.)

Based on this action alone, college administrators will either go screaming back into negotiations with their teachers and take actions to improve success rates, or face reductions in revenue that will force their successors to do so.

3. Develop & publicize college and course ranking metrics relevant to educational success.

Over the course of many decades, wealthier nations have contributed billions of dollars to various poor countries in efforts to develop those countries and eradicate poverty. In some of those cases the efforts seemed to have positive results.

In other cases, billions and billions of dollars did not seem to contribute to the development of societies with less corrupt governments, and where the development of Western-style middle classes seemed perpetually stalled.

Rather than either repeat the same mistakes or give up altogether, a series of studies were conducted by the World Bank to determine what the successful efforts had in common that were missing from the failures. The studies examined how each aid program was implemented.

The results of these studies were not what the researchers had thought were most important. It didn't seem to matter if governments were Democratic or dictatorships or religious theocracies. In all of those cases there were developmental successes and failures. It didn't seem to matter which had formerly been colonies of which European powers. From whether there was a history of successful business or education levels or receptiveness to outside help, examples of success and failure abound.

It turned out that there was one differentiator that resulted in more success than failure in every instance. That differentiator was transparency. Any time a mechanism was put in place to publicly disclose where every dollar was spent, force naturally arose to reduce corruption and improve the development of productive economies that benefited the greatest number of people. Transparency in finance. Transparency in program results. Transparency in who was doing what and in what way. In the age of the internet, the ability to quickly and cost effectively put transparent systems in place only depends on the amount of resistance put up by those people being held accountable to achieve results. (154)

We can be inspired by both the experience of the U.S. Lemon Law and the findings of the African Aid Analysis to create a College educational system that is transparent, accountable, and ultimately, MUCH more successful than the system currently in place.

The approach I am advocating combines independent testing, transparency through public disclosure of results, and holding colleges accountable for the results of their education offerings. This approach recognizes that students (and the U.S. Government) are paying good money not for research, but for educational results; and the results currently experienced are not acceptable. The "blame the customer" mentality will no longer be accepted as a shield for colleges to avoid accountability.

There will be some colleges who protest such visibility and accountability by citing violations of their "academic freedoms." Some may decry a loss of independent thought as the result of ever more course standardization. In fact, their concerns will be valid. But those concerns are not the concerns of the tuition paying family whose offspring are destined for a STEM career. I would not be surprised if college teaching careers split into two very different career tracks.

One track might be professors who are paid through private and government grants to do research. A completely different career track that rewards teachers with the best teaching skill and which drive out the few who are not good teachers.

The many competing college ranking systems presented to the public today are confusing, often take into account irrelevant factors, and their calculation is often a mystery to the public, as well as to prospective students and their families.

The following sections discuss what should be measured and how the measures should be quantified and publicized.

In a prior section, I referred to how in 2015, Michigan State University's Professor Steve Hsu and, Duke University's Jonathan Wai published an article in which they attempted to rank colleges based on their contributions to science, society and technology.

If all we want to do is to congratulate the colleges on their contributions to society, their list has a purpose. But this (and competing lists) border on meaninglessness if I am a STEM student.

If we want them to succeed, metrics each STEM student should focus should be related to helping them understand the quality of education offered by each college.

In the context of this book, a student needs to know the following:

1. Based on the results of independent post-course mastery exams, what percentage of students at that college IN MY MAJOR graduate in six years?

2. Are the success statistics for all teachers public and can I choose my teachers when registering for courses?

3. What are the limitations and restrictions on transferring courses from other colleges?

Note that I did not even mention, "Were the dorms crowded, old, and yucky?" I did not note school spirit, quality of food, quality of athletic facilities, or any other item not related to their future. I also did not note "How many Noble Prizes have been earned by the college's teachers," or "How many patents have those teachers earned?"

That doesn't mean a student is a bad person if they DO think about these things. But they need to consider them only AFTER considering the more important questions.

By developing and publicizing measures reflecting these concerns, the government can accomplish two complementary goals.

First, students can be empowered to make more intelligent college selection choices.

Second, when college administrators realize that students are making college selection decisions based on these measures, they can either focus on improving their educational offerings or face the consequences of ignoring their customers' decisions.

The National College Activity Database

By requiring colleges to report a small amount of data to a proposed **National College Activity Database**, a great deal of information can be determined with respect to all of the questions in this book. A college who fails to comply with reporting requirements would not be eligible for their students to receive government backed student loans.

I am proposing the creation of a cloud-based system that would enable both manual and automated system to capture student registration, teacher ID, pre-requisite test score, final test results, and major changes and study interruptions.

Based on this information, we may then regularly publish

- Percent of students in each major who fail or change major in the first four years

- Percent of students in each major who graduate in six years

- Percent of students who forfeit any or all scholarship

The data will also enable the publication that not only rates schools and majors, but success percentages for each course and rough competence ratings down to the teacher level.

College Overall Proficiency: This calculation begins by colleges reporting the number of students enrolled as freshmen for the first time at their college in a calendar year. This includes both full time and part time students, matriculated and non-matriculated. If a non-matriculated student registers for a course generally associated with STEM majors, they will be considered to be a STEM major.

Examining the prior 16 years, what percentage of students admitted as freshmen (or took their first course having previously earned 30 or fewer credits elsewhere), completed their degree within 6 years.

For example, if a college admitted 100 STEM freshmen in calendar 2010 and 20 of those students successfully earned their Bachelor of Science degree by December of 2016, that college scores a 20% Graduation Proficiency © grade.

If that college admitted 100 STEM freshmen in calendar 2010 and 80 of those students successfully earned their Bachelor of Science degree by December of 2016, that college scores an 80% Graduation Proficiency © grade.

Metrics Example 1 – College Education Proficiency

Admission Year	Freshman Class	Measured Graduation Year	B.S. Awarded	% Graduated in 6 Years
2001	100	2007	50	50%
2002	100	2007	49	49%
2003	100	2007	40	40%
2004	100	2007	50	50%
2005	100	2007	56	56%
2006	100	2007	60	60%
2007	100	2007	48	48%
2008	100	2007	62	62%
2009	100	2007	50	50%
2010	100	2007	48	48%
	1000		513	51%

In the above example, we score a mythical college based on its ten-year track record. Over that period, 1,000 students were admitted to study B.S. programs. 51% were awarded their degree in six years. If a student earned any other degree, they do not count in this metric. If a student left the college for any reason and then graduated with a B.S. from any other suitably accredited college, then this college WOULD count that student as a success. In this way, even two-year colleges can be scored and ranked.

By using the prior ten years as the measure, we may also detect trends where a college is improving or deteriorating with regard to their educational effectiveness. A ten-year measurement also provides a larger sample so that even smaller colleges can be effectively scored.

4. Tie Borrowing Limits to Expected Outcomes

Tuition Inflation and the effect of Intelligent Limiting of Tuition Loans

The premise of this book is that the principal reason for a student to go to college and study for a STEM career is that it should make financial sense to do so. Most of the text has been focused on reducing failure rates. Now we will examine why we need to control the cost of college.

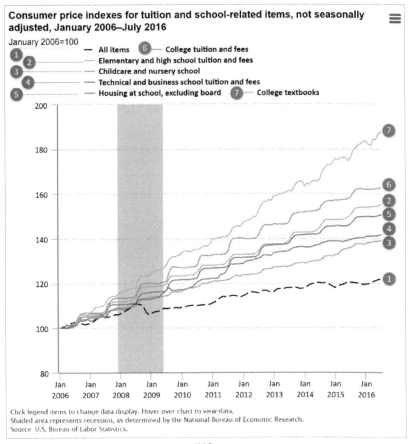

Consumer price indexes for tuition and school-related items, not seasonally adjusted, January 2006–July 2016

Click legend items to change data display. Hover over chart to view data.
Shaded area represents recession, as determined by the National Bureau of Economic Research.
Source: U.S. Bureau of Labor Statistics.

(115)

In an era of flat or slowly rising incomes, the cost of college tuition and fees has relentlessly outpaced inflation since the turn of the century.

Some may argue that by increasing the pool of money available for college loans, that the lenders (now primarily, but not limited to the federal government,) are to blame. Their position has been that by increasing the amount of borrowable funds, that colleges have raced to build fancy cafeterias and sports arenas and exercise facilities as those are what students see on their tours and often use as a basis to choose their college.

A friend of mine took his daughter to tour Rowan University as the college offered the biomedical engineering program she will be pursuing somewhere. The tour started with the old, crowded, and run-down dorms that freshman are stuck with.

That the rest of the college has beautiful dorms, labs, and engineering facilities and that the college has classrooms with less than forty students, zero lecture halls for STEM students, were all topics that were suddenly irrelevant.

Ten minutes in the cramped, hot, gloomy freshman dorm and she ruled out attending Rowan EVER. (While as of this writing Rowan has many new dorms under construction, I am not aware of any plans to rehabilitate or discontinue use of the old dorms.) Fairleigh Dickenson University in Teaneck, New Jersey, suffers from the same "ugly dorm syndrome."

Can you blame the administrators nationwide for embarking on upgrading our colleges to become ever more luxurious?

In a 2013 study of 925 not-for-profit colleges, [19] Forbes magazine judged 107 schools to have a financial rating of "D" or worse. There are many administrators who understand fully that those colleges with declining enrollment either turn around their competitive positions or they will fail.

The problem today, is that students are focusing on short-term comforts instead of college qualities that will insure them long term career success.

In order to balance the financing needs of the student with the desire not to unduly burden them with debt, we can first look at mortgages, the United States' largest and most mature consumer market for debt.

From the government website: [22]

In order to prevent homebuyers from getting into a home they cannot afford, FHA requirements and guidelines have been set in place requiring borrowers and/or their spouse to qualify according to set debt to income ratios. These ratios are used to calculate whether or not the potential borrower is in a financial position that would allow them to meet the demands that are often included in owning a home.

The two ratios are as follows:

1) Mortgage Payment Expense to Effective Income: Add up the total mortgage payment (principal and interest, escrow deposits for taxes, hazard insurance, mortgage insurance premium, homeowners' dues, etc.). Then, take that amount and divide it by the gross monthly income. The maximum ratio to qualify is 31%.

2) Total Fixed Payment to Effective Income: Add up the total mortgage payment (principal and interest, escrow deposits for taxes, hazard insurance, mortgage insurance premium,

homeowners' dues, etc.) and all recurring monthly revolving and installment debt (car loans, personal loans, student loans, credit cards, etc.). Then, take that amount and divide it by the gross monthly income. The maximum ratio to qualify is 43%. (22)

The reason for adhering to these limits are that studies have shown that borrowers who stay within these limits are less likely to default on loans. (21)

A Bankrate.com article in 2011 (20) and the Detroit Free Press in 2016 (72) repeated traditional advice on limiting college debt. They advised that one not borrow more money than one expects to earn the first year out of college.

According to that article, an engineering graduate who can expect their starting salary to be $70,000 should not be permitted to borrow more than $70,000.

According to that article, a Graphic Arts student studying to become a Graphic Design Specialist should expect a starting salary of about $42,000. They should not be permitted to borrow more than $42,000.

I'm not sure that I agree with such stringent limits.

But consider someone who majors in Marketing to become a Marketing Specialist. Based on data from Salary.com (152), they can expect to earn
$48,000 in their first year and $66,000 by the fifth year of their career. For that person to borrow $240,000 is just not in their best interests or the interests of society.

I suggest we consider double their expected fifth year earnings as a borrowing cap.

However, the government's web site does not even mention the major as a consideration in loan limitations. [121]

The U.S. Department of Labor annually publishes wage statics for more than 800 professions. Salary.com provides a similar service. Students need to be educated about the relationship of the amount of money they borrow to the amount of money they will reasonably be expected to pay back over time. Based on the current default rates, we are failing to educate students about this very important metric.

The impact of these limitations may be to focus students on considering lower cost options for obtaining their degree. Some students who today turn up their noses at spending their first two years at community colleges or taking online courses at a school like Thomas Edison University, might reconsider their options if they really focused on their ability to repay their college loans.

When I say "permitted to borrow," I am saying from all sources other than their families. Private loans that practically create a near-lifetime class of indentured serfs, should be regulated and discouraged as long as there are lower cost alternatives to private schools who, after discounting list prices, are still charging $42,000 per year after including room, board, and textbooks. These additional private loans are no different than the sub-prime mortgage industry who, in the early part of this century, made sub-prime mortgage loans to millions of people who had no reasonable expectation of ever being able to repay those loans.

In fact, even the most impoverished students may be able to afford a bachelor's degree using these guidelines coupled with today's need-based scholarship programs. But more of them may need to choose lower cost options during their college career.

Fortunately, as the prior chapter's discussion on college reputation illustrated, for most their education will be just as good and their incomes just as good as long as they choose properly accredited institutions.

5. Incentivize Schools without Credit Transfer Limits

Just as there are colleges that will continue to require students to live on-campus, there will always be some colleges that will not open their market of courses to competition from other schools. While colleges such as Excelsior, Charter Oak, and Thomas Edison have demonstrated they can thrive in an open market, I do not expect the majority of colleges to easily give up the guaranteed revenue that comes from such an approach.

Assuming that the courses in a college that students elect to take elsewhere are a minority, I would suggest that continued loans be conditioned on two criteria:

1) Colleges must allow students to transfer or obtain credit-by-exam for up to 50% of all courses that apply to their STEM degree.

2) Colleges may not require any specific STEM course be taken at their institution.

If a college is so protective of its monopoly of courses that it will not implement these rules, then that college can do so without their students able to borrow from the government.

6. Legislate Advisor Fiduciary Responsibility

In the world of finance, there are many individuals who market themselves as "Financial Advisors." Some of the products sold by many Financial Advisors include stocks, bonds, life insurance, annuities, and all manner of retirement, savings, and other investment accounts.

Funny thing, while their customers often assumed that their "Financial Advisor" was providing advice in their customer's best interest, in fact an unacceptably large percentage sold their customers financial instruments with enormous commissions for the Financial Advisor that were really not in the customer's best interest at all.

In 2016, the Obama administration implemented regulations requiring financial advisors to recommend investments that are in their client's (not the advisor's) best interests. (84)

While the subsequent Trump administration moved to roll back these regulations, the issue of financial advisors pushing the wrong investments is still a topic of concern for many legislators.

So, the legislative battle is whether someone who sells you a life insurance policy that could cost you one hundred dollars a month for ten years should only sell you a policy that is in your best interest, whether or not that policy brings the greatest commission to the salesperson's employer.

Consider that college "recruiters" and "advisors" are selling something that can plunge their customer hundreds of thousands of dollars in debt, and that their customers are, by definition, not sophisticated investors or consumers. Isn't it time we passed a law or regulation obligating those recruiters or advisors to provide advice that is in the best interest of the student even if that advice may be to go to school elsewhere? I think so.

7. Improving Teacher Quality

There has been much written about how many, if not most colleges, have reduced the number of full-time tenured teachers in favor of the part-time "adjunct" teacher. Some proponents of this trend argue that some part-time teachers bring actual work experience into the classroom as opposed to the "ivory tower" mentality of some professors. Another reason used by proponents is that administrators can quickly identify and replace adjuncts if the quality of their teaching is shown to be lacking. This contrasts with some teachers who hide behind tenure and "academic freedom" to provide an inferior teaching service.

The real reason for most colleges to pursue this trend is simple economics. The total compensation paid to adjuncts after considering all benefits, salary, vacation, retirement accounts, etc. is dramatically less than the compensation paid to full-time tenure tenured teachers. For example, one of my daughters taught college English at a regionally accredited college for eight years. She taught a full course-load, advised on the college newspaper, and supervised student activities as well. This meant she worked forty-five to sixty hours per week year-round. (This college offered courses and activities through the summer.) Her compensation? Twenty-two thousand dollars per year with no health care, no paid time off, and no retirement account.

Yet the college charged their students the exact same amount of tuition for courses taught by adjuncts as those taught by tenured full-time teachers.

In a perfect world, teachers' unions nationwide would strike a deal that balances the needs of ALL teachers with the interests of the students who are their customers.

Unfortunately, my understanding of the U.S. Labor Laws is that they have been limited to prevent exactly that kind of action. (106)

Instead, I would suggest that the unions work with the regional accreditation authorities to implement teacher compensation standards as part of the accreditation process.

Such a deal would recognize that colleges are offering a service, and that their student-customers are no longer captive audiences who will accept anything less than the best teaching service. At the same time, teachers whose students perform well on independent national exams will likely attract more students to their classes and ultimately, more to the college as well.

As a result, total teacher compensation will be the same on a course-by course basis, regardless of employment status. Teaching will be seen as a service funded by tuition.

Teachers whose students do poorly on independent national exams will be quickly "released" from teaching duties, or their compensation will reflect the number of students willing to take their course. This approach is capitalism and the free-market truly at work. It makes teachers (and their employers) accountable to their student-customers.

It should also increase the compensation on the low-end to adjuncts, while also increasing compensation at the high end to those exceptional teachers who attract more customers for their services.

I would suggest legislation authorizing regional accreditation authorities to work with teacher unions and colleges to set national minimum compensation standards that set a level playing field for colleges and stops the "race to the bottom" that drives down teacher compensation while at the same time keeping STEM student failures unacceptably high.

Afterword

You made to the end! Thank you. I wrote this book because I wanted to help people address the many problems of STEM education as it is practiced today. That you got this far tells me another person is willing to be part of the solution.

You now have tools to be part of the solution.

If you are a student, you know the questions to ask and actions to take to avoid becoming part of the fifty percent who fail to get the degree they want in their desired STEM profession.

If you are a parent, you know how to advise your offspring so they may avoid being trapped in debt and in a career where they are miserable.

If you are a legislator, you have the information you can use to incent colleges to improve.

If you are a guidance counselor, librarian, or teacher, you have a resource that will better guide your STEM students than any they currently use.

If you are a taxpayer and/or U.S. resident, the quantity of scientists, doctors, engineers, and others who will serve you, serve society, and pay more taxes, depends on actions our legislators need to take. You are now a more informed voter. Fixing this system is not currently a top priority for our legislators. You might be surprised at what a few more emails and phone calls might do to change the conversation.

ANOTHER SHAMELESS PLUG

If you found this book to be of value, please say so in a review on Amazon.com or BarnesAndNobel.com. Your positive reviews are what will spread the word and the messages within this book.

If you are part of an organization who contracts for speakers, my contact information is at www.**TheSTEMStudentSurvivalGuide.com**.

I am also available as an "expert witness" to testify before government committees and other policy bodies.
Thank you for being part of the solution.

Mailing List? Twitter?

Want to hear from me as I travel the country and advocate for better treatment of STEM students? I send a single monthly email reporting news and corrections about the subjects discussed in this book. To sign up, register at www.thestemstudentsurvivalguide.com/feedback. **(I never share your email with others.)**

Images on this page: (162)

Notes and References

(1) Website: *Salary.Com*. No article title, author or publication date available. (Accessed 05/30/2016). <http://swz.salary.com/SalaryWizard/Pharmacist-Salary-Details.aspx> (Query: Job Title: Pharmacist)

(2) Website: *Gallup.Com*. Article Title: **Honesty/Ethics in Professions**. No author available. Publication Date: 02/06/2015. (Accessed 05/30/2016). < http://www.gallup.com/poll/1654/honesty-ethics-professions.aspx>

As per Gallup Permissions Department: Copyright © 2015 Gallup, Inc. All rights reserved. The content is used with permission; however, Gallup retains all rights of republication.

(3) Website: *Pharmaceutical Society of Singapore*. **The Many Faces of Pharmacists**. No article author or publication date available. (Accessed 5/30/2016). <http://www.pss.org.sg/about-pharmacists>

(4) Website: *Redfish technology*. **Hot Tech Salary and Trend Highlights**. No article author available. Published 4/18/2013. (Accessed 7/12/2016). <http://www.redfishtech.com/2013/04/18/hot-tech-salary-and-trend-highlights-2013/> (Summarizes, references and links to Robert Half study.)

(5) Website: *Infoplease.com*. **Number of U.S. Colleges and Universities and Degrees Awarded, 2005**. No article author or publication date available. (Accessed 7/12/2016). < http://www.infoplease.com/ipa/A0908742.html>

(6) Website: *Quartz at qz.com*. **These 25 schools are responsible for the greatest advances in science**. Authors: Steve Hsu, Jonathan Wai. Published 9/10/2015. (Accessed 7/12/2016). < http://qz.com/498534/these-25-schools-are-responsible-for-the-greatest-advances-in-science/>

(7) Website: *PsychCentral at psychcentral.com*. **Even Brief Meditation Can Improve Student Performance**. Author: Rick Nauert, PhD. No publication date available. (Accessed 7/12/2016). <http://psychcentral.com/news/2013/04/10/even-brief-meditation-can-

improve-student-performance/53645.html> (Summarizes research from the journal, *Mindfulness*.)

(8) Website: *Florida National University at fnu.edu.* **The Link Between Sports and Academic Performance**. Author: Scott J. Schmidt. Published 3/18/2014. (Accessed 7/12/2016). < http://www.fnu.edu/the-link-between-sports-and-academic-performance/>

(9) Website: *Excelsior College at excelsior.edu.* Title: **Costs & Financing**. No author or publication date available. (Accessed 7/12/2016). <http://www.excelsior.edu/costs-and-financing>

(10) Website: *Thomas Edison State University at tesu.edu.* Title: **Transferring Your Credit**. No author or publication date available. (Accessed 7/12/2016). < http://www.tesu.edu/admissions/Transfer-Credit.cfm>

(11) Website: **Thomas Edison State University**. (2016, June 11). *In Wikipedia, The Free Encyclopedia*. Retrieved 16:45, July 12, 2016, from:<https://en.wikipedia.org/w/index.php?title=Thomas_Edison_State_University&oldid=724792928>

(12) Website: **Charter Oak State College**. (2016, May 11). *In Wikipedia, The Free Encyclopedia*. Retrieved 16:49, July 12, 2016, from <https://en.wikipedia.org/w/index.php?title=Charter_Oak_State_College&oldid=719801138>

(13) Website: *College Board at collegeboard.org.* **SAT Percentile Ranks for Males, Females, and Total Group**. No author or publication date available. (Accessed 7/12/2016). <https://secure-media.collegeboard.org/digitalServices/pdf/sat/sat-percentile-ranks-composite-crit-reading-math-writing-2014.pdf>

(14) Website: *National Public Radio at npr.org.* **For First Time In 130 Years, More Young Adults Live With Parents Than With Partners**. Author: Camila Domonoske. Published 5/24/2016. (Accessed 7/12/2016). < http://www.npr.org/sections/thetwo-way/2016/05/24/479327382/for-first-time-in-130-years-more-young-adults-live-with-parents-than-partners>

(15) Website: *USA Today at usatoday.com*. **College student's nightmare: Loan debt and no degree**. Author: Susan Tompor. Published 6/7/2015. (Accessed 7/12/2016). < http://www.usatoday.com/story/money/columnist/tompor/tompor/2015/06/07/student-loans-repay-delinquency-federal-reserve/28562447/>

(16) Website: *Federal Reserve Bank of New York at newyorkfed.org*. Speech Title: **Rising Household Borrowing**. Author: James J. McAndrews. Published: 3/6/2014. (Accessed 7/12/2016). Speech URL:<https://www.newyorkfed.org/newsevents/speeches/2014/mca140306> Chart Title : **Total Debt Balance and Its Composition.** Chart URL:https://www.newyorkfed.org/medialibrary/media/newsevents/speeches/2014/mca140306_14.pdf

(17) Website: *Student Debt Relief at studentdebtrelief.us*. **Rising Tuition Costs and the History of Student Loans**. Author: Demetrios Sourmaidis. Published: November 7, 2013. (Accessed 7/12/2016). <http://www.studentdebtrelief.us/news/rising-tuition-costs-and-the-history-of-student-loans/>

(18) Website: *College Board at collegeboard.org*. **Trends in Higher Education. Average Published Undergraduate Charges by Sector, 2015-16**. No available author or publication date. (Accessed 7/12/2016). <https://trends.collegeboard.org/college-pricing/figures-tables/average-published-undergraduate-charges-sector-2015-16>

(19) Website: **Forbes at forbes.com. Is Your College Going Broke? The Most And Least Financially Fit Schools In America**. Author: Matt Schifrin. Published 8/13/13. (Accessed 7/12/2016). <http://www.forbes.com/sites/schifrin/2013/07/24/is-your-college-going-broke/#3402346768c6>

(20) Website: *Bankrate.com*. **3 Tips To Limit Student Debt**. Author: Marilyn Kennedy Melia. No publication date. (Accessed 7/12/2016). <http://www.bankrate.com/finance/college-finance/payback-3-tips-to-manage-student-loans-1.aspx>

(21) Website: *Consumer Financial Protection Bureau at http://www.consumerfinance.gov/*. **What is a debt-to-income ratio? Why is the 43% debt-to-income ratio important?** No author or publication date. (Accessed 7/12/2016).

<http://www.consumerfinance.gov/askcfpb/1791/what-debt-income-ratio-why-43-debt-income-ratio-important.html>

(22) Website: *Federal Housing Administration at fha.com.* **FHA Requirements - Debt-to-Income Ratio Guidelines**. No author or publication date. (Accessed 7/12/2016).
<http://www.fha.com/fha_requirements_debt>

(23) Website: *Salary.Com.* No article title, author or publication date available. (Accessed 05/30/2016).
<http://swz.salary.com/SalaryWizard/Pharmacist-Salary-Details.aspx> (Query: Job Title: Graphic Design Specialist)

(33) Website: *The Washington Post at washintonpost.com.* **The great grade deflation experiment, STEM vs. humanities**. Author: Catherine Rampell. Published: August 12, 2014. (Accessed 7/12/2016).
<https://www.washingtonpost.com/news/rampage/wp/2014/08/12/the-great-grade-deflation-experiment-stem-vs-humanities/>

(34) Website: *New York Time Economix Blogs at economix.blogs.nytimes.com.* **College Majors Matter**. Author: Catherine Rampell. Published: 11/2/2011. (Accessed 7/12/2016).
<http://economix.blogs.nytimes.com/2011/11/02/college-majors-matter/?_r=0>

(35) Website: *The Wall Street Journal at wsj.com.* **Need Additional Loans for College? Consider These Options**. Author: Veronica Dagher Published: June 10, 2016. (Accessed 7/12/2016).
<http://www.wsj.com/articles/need-additional-loans-for-college-consider-these-options-1465551000>

(36) Website: *PrepScholar at http://blog.prepscholar.com.* **What's the Average College GPA? By Major?** Author: Samantha Lindsay. Published: Aug 7, 2015. (Accessed 7/12/2016).
<http://blog.prepscholar.com/average-college-gpa-by-major>

(37) Website: *ITT Technical Institute at itt-tech.edu.* **Net Price Calculator**. No author or publication date. (Accessed 7/12/2016).
<https://www.itt-tech.edu/npc/> (Entered parameters: Yes to Financial Aid, Yes to Housing, 18 for Age, Yes for Financial Aid.)

(38) Web Site: *ATT: at attn.com*. **The Graduation Rate of For-Profit Colleges is Shocking**. SEPTEMBER 20TH 2014By: Lindsay Haskell. (Accessed 7/12/2016). <http://www.attn.com/stories/118/graduation-rate-profit-colleges-shocking>

(39) Website: *QuotationsPage.com*. **Quotation #26032 from Michael Moncur's (Cynical) Quotations**. Author: Michael Moncur. No publication date. (Accessed 7/12/2016). <http://www.quotationspage.com/quote/26032.html>

(40) Website: *Rasansky Law Firm*. **ITT Technical Institute Scam**. No author available. Published 12/16/2013. (Accessed 7/12/2016). http://www.schoolscamlawyer.com/college-accreditation-fraud/

(41) Website: *Forbes at forbes.com*. **More Than Half of College Faculty Are Adjuncts: Should You Care?** Author: Dan Edmonds. Published 5/28/2015. (Accessed 7/12/2016). <http://www.forbes.com/sites/noodleeducation/2015/05/28/more-than-half-of-college-faculty-are-adjuncts-should-you-care/#262443681d9b>

(42) Website: *American Association of University Professors at aaup.org*. **Background Facts on Contingent Faculty**. No author of publication date available. Accessed 7/12/2016) <https://www.aaup.org/issues/contingency/background-facts>.

(43) Website: *The Atlantic at theatlantic.com*. **The Ever-Shrinking Role of Tenured College Professors (in 1 Chart)**. Author: Jordan Weissmann. Published: Apr 10, 2013. (Accessed 7/12/2016). <http://www.theatlantic.com/business/archive/2013/04/the-ever-shrinking-role-of-tenured-college-professors-in-1-chart/274849/>

The chart referenced by the Atlantic Article is in this document: https://www.aaup.org/sites/default/files/files/AAUP_Report_InstrStaff-75-11_apr2013.pdf

(44) Website*: Excelsior College at Excelsior.edu*. **About Excelsior College – Philosophy**. No author or publication date available. (Accessed 7/12/2016). <http://www.excelsior.edu/about>

(45) Website: *Salary.Com*. No article title, author or publication date available. (Accessed 05/30/2016).

<http://swz.salary.com/SalaryWizard/Pharmacist-Salary-Details.aspx> (Query: Job Title: Professor - Mathematics)

(46) Website: (42) Website: *American Association of University Professors at aaup.org*. **Background Facts on Contingent Faculty**. No author of publication date available. (Accessed 7/12/2016). https://www.aaup.org/sites/default/files/files/AAUP_Report_InstrStaff-75-11_apr2013.pdf

(47) Website: *Washington Post @ washingtonpost.com*. **College courses without textbooks? These schools are giving it a shot.** Author: Danielle Douglas-Gabriel June 15 2016. (Accessed 7/12/2016). <https://www.washingtonpost.com/news/grade-point/wp/2016/06/15/college-courses-without-textbooks-these-schools-are-giving-it-a-shot/>

(48) Website: *Washington Post @ washingtonpost.com*. **Freshman residency rules sometimes force students to pay prohibitive costs**. Author: Danielle Douglas-Gabriel. Published: September 29, 2015. (Accessed 7/12/2016). <https://www.washingtonpost.com/local/education/freshman-residency-rules-sometimes-force-students-to-pay-prohibitive-costs/2015/09/29/4693aed6-63b5-11e5-b38e-06883aacba64_story.html>

(49) Website: *CBSnews.com*. **5 hardest and easiest college majors by GPA's**. Author: Lynn O'Shaughnessy. Last Updated Apr 15, 2010 7:03 PM EDT. (Accessed 7/1/2016) <http://www.cbsnews.com/news/5-hardest-and-easiest-college-majors-by-gpas/>

(50) Website: *The Economist at economist.com*. **The disposable academic**. (Originally published in the print edition.) No author available. Published Dec 16th 2010. (Accessed 7/12/2016) <http://www.economist.com/node/17723223>

 (61) Website: LiveScience.com. Memory-Boosting Trick: Exercise After Learning. Author: Cari Nierenberg. Published 6/16/2016. (Accessed 7/12/2016). <http://www.livescience.com/55095-exercise-helps-you-retain-new-info.html>

(62) Website: *American Gap Association at americangap.org. **Gap Year Data & Benefits**. No author or publication date. <http://www.americangap.org/data-benefits.php>

(63) Website: *National Public Radio at npr.org.* **Brain Maturity Extends Well Beyond Teen Years**. Host: Tony Cox. Published 10/10/2011. (Accessed 7/12/2016). <http://www.npr.org/templates/story/story.php?storyId=141164708>

(64) Website: *Mentalhealthdaily.com.* **At What Age Is the Brain Fully Developed?** No author available. Published 2/18/2015. (Accessed 7/12/2016). <http://mentalhealthdaily.com/2015/02/18/at-what-age-is-the-brain-fully-developed/>

(65) Website: *The Wall Street Journal at wsj.com.* **Delayed Development: 20-Somethings Blame the Brain**. Author: Melinda Beck. Updated Aug. 23, 2012. (Accessed 7/12/2016). <http://www.wsj.com/articles/SB10000872396390443713704577601532208760746>

(66) Website: **Jean Piaget**. (2016, July 12). *In Wikipedia, The Free Encyclopedia*. Retrieved 00:20, July 13, 2016, from https://en.wikipedia.org/w/index.php?title=Jean_Piaget&oldid=729507237

(68) Website: *Wall Street Journal at wsj.com.* **To Get Doctors to Do the Right Thing, Try Comparing Them to Their Peers**. Author: Laura Landro Published: June 26, 2016. (Accessed 7/12/2016). <http://www.wsj.com/articles/to-get-doctors-to-do-the-right-thing-try-comparing-them-to-their-peers-1466993340>

(69) Website: **Ralph Nader**. (2016, June 20). *In Wikipedia, The Free Encyclopedia*. Retrieved 00:30, July 13, 2016, from https://en.wikipedia.org/w/index.php?title=Ralph_Nader&oldid=726244393

(71) Website: **Invisible hand**. (2016, June 8). *In Wikipedia, The Free Encyclopedia*. Retrieved 00:36, July 13, 2016, from <https://en.wikipedia.org/w/index.php?title=Invisible_hand&oldid=724271420>

(72) Website: *Detroit Free Press at freep.com*. **College debt, no degree means world of financial hurt**. Author: Susan Tompor. Published June 30, 2016. (Accessed 7/12/2016). <http://www.freep.com/story/money/personal-finance/susan-tompor/2016/06/29/college-debt-whats-too-much/86464144/>

(73) Website: *American Association of University Professors - American Federation of Teachers AFL-CIO at rutgersaaup.org*. No author or publication date. (Accessed 7/12/2016). **The "Awful Truth" about Non-Tenure Track Faculty Salaries**. <http://www.rutgersaaup.org/documents/awful-truth-about-non-tenure-track-faculty-salaries> Charts: <http://rutgersaaup.org/sites/default/files/images/NTT-Document-on-salary-02-14-13.pdf>

(75) Website: *Wallethub.com*. **2016's Property Taxes by State**. Author: John S Kiernan. No publication date. (Accessed 7/12/2016). <https://wallethub.com/edu/states-with-the-highest-and-lowest-property-taxes/11585/>

(76) Website: *247wallst.com*. **States Paying the Highest (and Lowest) Taxes**. Authors: Thomas C. Frohlich and Michael B. Sauter. Published: January 21, 2016. (Accessed 7/12/2016). <http://247wallst.com/special-report/2016/01/21/states-paying-the-highest-and-lowest-taxes/>

(77) Website: *Huffington Post at huffingtonpost.com*. **9 Reasons Why Being an Adjunct Faculty Member Is Terrible**. Author: Tyler Kingkade. Published 11/11/2013. (Accessed 7/12/2016). <http://www.huffingtonpost.com/2013/11/11/adjunct-faculty_n_4255139.html>

(78) Website: *Bureau of Labor Statistics at bls.gov*. **Occupational Employment and Wages, May 2015 - 25-1191 Graduate Teaching Assistants**. No author. No publication date. (Accessed 7/12/2016). <http://www.bls.gov/oes/current/oes251191.htm>

(80) Website: *The Hechinger Report at hechingerreport.org*. **High failure rates spur universities to overhaul math class**. Author: Karen Shakerdge. Published: 5/6/2016. (Accessed 7/12/2016). <http://hechingerreport.org/high-failure-rates-spur-universities-overhaul-math-class/>

(82) Website: *University of Washington at Washington.edu.* **Improve grades, reduce failure – undergrads should tell profs 'Don't lecture me.'** Author: Sandra Hines. Published 5/12/2014. (Accessed 7/12/2016). <http://www.washington.edu/news/2014/05/12/improve-grades-reduce-failure-undergrads-should-tell-profs-dont-lecture-me/>

(84) Website: *The New York Times at nytimes.com.* **'Customers First' to Become the Law in Retirement Investing.** Author: Tara Siegel Bernard. Published: April 6, 2016. (Accessed 7/12/2016) <http://www.nytimes.com/2016/04/07/your-money/new-rules-for-retirement-accounts-financial-advisers.html?_r=1>

(87) Website: *Bloomberg News at Bloomberg.com.* **America's Unwanted Ivy Leaguers Are Flocking to India**. Author: Dina Bass. Published: 6/2/2015. (Accessed 7/13/2016). <http://www.bloomberg.com/news/articles/2015-06-02/chasing-the-american-dream-in-india >

(88) Huiyao Wang and Yue Bao (Authors), **Reverse Migration in Contemporary China: Returnees, Entrepreneurship and the Chinese Economy (Politics and Development of Contemporary China) Kindle Edition**. First published in 2015 by Palgrace Macmillan. ISBN 978-1-137-45059-3.

(90) Website: *Massachusetts Budget and Policy Center at massbudget.org.* **Who is Affected by the Minimum Wage?** Author: Sarah Nolan. Published June 1, 2012 (updated: January 18, 2013). (Accessed 7/13/2016) <http://www.massbudget.org/report_window.php?loc=minimum_wage_effects.html>

(91) Website: *ICEF Monitor at monitor.icef.com.* **China and India to produce 40% of global graduates by 2020**. No author available. Published 6/16/2012. (Accessed 7/13/2016). <http://monitor.icef.com/2012/07/china-and-india-to-produce-40-of-global-graduates-by-2020/>

(92) Website: *marginalrevolution.com.* **College has been oversold.** Author; Alex Tabarrok. Published November 2, 2011. (Accessed 7/13/2016).

<http://marginalrevolution.com/marginalrevolution/2011/11/college-has-been-oversold.html>

(93) Website: *Science Magazine at sciencemag.org*. **Data check: U.S. producing more STEM graduates even without proposed initiatives**. Author: Jeffrey Mervis. Published: Jun. 30, 2014. (Accessed 7/13/2016). <http://www.sciencemag.org/news/2014/06/data-check-us-producing-more-stem-graduates-even-without-proposed-initiatives.

(95) Website: *U.S. Department of Education at ed.gov*. **The College Payoff**. Authors: Anthony P. Carnevale, Stephen J. Rose, and Ban Cheah. Attached PDF Document: <https://www2.ed.gov/policy/highered/reg/hearulemaking/2011/collegepayoff.pdf>

(96) *Office of the President of the United States at whitehouse.gov*. **One Decade, One Million more STEM Graduates**. Author: Michael Feder. Published December 18, 2012. (Accessed 7/13/2016). <https://www.whitehouse.gov/blog/2012/12/18/one-decade-one-million-more-stem-graduates>

(99) Website: *The Drucker Institute at druckerinstitute.com*. **Measurement Myopia**. Author: Paul Zak. Published 7/4/2013. (Accessed 7/13/2016). http://www.druckerinstitute.com/2013/07/measurement-myopia/

(100) Website: *Kaiser Health News at khn.org*. **Medicare to Penalize 2,217 Hospitals For Excess Readmissions**. Author: Jordan Rau. Published: August 13, 2012. (Accessed 7/13/2016). <http://khn.org/news/medicare-hospitals-readmissions-penalties/>

(101) Website: *Kaiser Health News at khn.org*. **Medicare Fines 2,610 Hospitals in Third Round of Readmission Penalties**. Author: Jordan Rau. Published: October 2, 2014. (Accessed 7/13/2016). <http://khn.org/news/medicare-readmissions-penalties-2015/>

(102) Website: *Kaiser Health News at khn.org*. **Half of Nation's Hospitals Fail Again to Escape Medicare's Readmission Penalties**. Author: Jordan Rau. Published: August 3, 2015. (Accessed 7/13/2016). <http://khn.org/news/half-of-nations-hospitals-fail-again-to-escape-medicares-readmission-penalties/>

(103) Website: *Executive Insight at advanceweb.com*. **Managing Hospital Readmissions**. Authors: Michelle Aurelio, MPH, Ray Wang, MS & Cary Sennett, MD, PhD. Published: March 14, 2011. (Accessed 7/13/2016). <http://healthcare-executive-insight.advanceweb.com/Features/Articles/Managing-Hospital-Readmissions.aspx>

(104) Adopted from: Website: Center on Education and the Workforce. **STEM**. Authors: Anthony P. Carnevale, Nichole Smith, Michelle Melton. (Accessed 6/24/2017). <https://cew.georgetown.edu/cew-reports/stem/#full-report>

(105) Website: Cipherhealth.com. What's Next for Readmissions? No author available. Published: 10/1/2014. Accessed 6/21/2017. <https://cipherhealth.com/whats-next-for-readmissions/>

(106) Website: *National Labor Relations Board at nlrb.gov*. **Secondary boycotts (Section 8(b)(4))**. No author or publication date available. (Accessed 7/13/2016). <https://www.nlrb.gov/rights-we-protect/whats-law/unions/secondary-boycotts-section-8b4>

(107) Website: *greyenlightenment.com*. **Improving Obama's Community College Plan**. No author or publication date available. Noted on web page: Monthly Archives: January 2015. (Accessed 7/13/2016). <http://greyenlightenment.com/2015/01/page/3/>

(109) Website: *The World Economic Forum at weforum.org*. **Are These the World's Best Jobs?** Author: Murray Nicol. Published Thursday 22 October 2015. (Accessed 7/13/2016). <https://www.weforum.org/agenda/2015/10/worlds-best-job-the-answer-might-surprise-you/>

(111) Website: *The New York Times at nytimes.com*. **Most College Students Don't Earn a Degree in 4 Years, Study Finds**. Author: Tamar Lewindec. Published: 12/1/2014. (Accessed 7/13/2016). <http://www.nytimes.com/2014/12/02/education/most-college-students-dont-earn-degree-in-4-years-study-finds.html?_r=1>

(112) Website: *collegefactual.com*. **Specialized Accreditations. Specialized Accreditations for University of Pennsylvania**. No author or publication date. (Accessed 7/13/2016).

<http://www.collegefactual.com/colleges/university-of-pennsylvania/academic-life/accreditation/>

(113) Website: *Engineering Degrees Online at typesofengineeringdegrees.org*. **3 Reasons for High Engineering School Dropout Rates**. Author: Michael L. Murray. No publication date. (Accessed 7/13/2016).
<http://typesofengineeringdegrees.org/engineering-school-dropout-rates/>

(114) Website: *USA Today at usatoday.com*. Survey: **Engineering seniors log the most study hours**. Author: Mary Beth Marklein. Updated 11/17/2011. (Accessed 7/13/2016).
<http://usatoday30.usatoday.com/news/education/story/2011-11-17/college-students-study-hours/51245162/1>

(115) Website: http://www.bls.gov. No cited author or date. Accessed 11/24/2016. **College tuition and fees increase 63 percent since January 2006**. https://www.bls.gov/opub/ted/2016/college-tuition-and-fees-increase-63-percent-since-january-2006.htm

(116) Website: *Statista at statista.com*. **The Countries Where Kids Do the Most Homework**. Author: Niall McCarthy, Published: Feb 19, 2015. (Accessed 7/13/2016).
<https://www.statista.com/chart/3242/the-countries-where-kids-do-the-most-homework/>

(118) Website: *www.gooverseas.com*. **Why Are Gap Years More Common in Europe than the US?** Author: Jennifer Moy. Published: 07/25/2013. (Accessed 7/13/2016).
https://www.gooverseas.com/blog/why-gap-years-more-common-in-europe-us

(119) Website: *Huffington Post at huffingtonpost.com*. **Apple Manufacturing in USA: CEO Tim Cook Shares Company's Plans to Make a Line of Macs in America**. Author: Catharine Smith. Updated Feb 05, 2013. (Accessed 7/13/2016)
<http://www.huffingtonpost.com/2012/12/06/apple-manufacturing-usa-macs_n_2249613.html>

(120) Website: *Pew Research Center at pewresearch.org*. **Increase in living with parents driven by those ages 25-34, non-college grads.**

Author: Drew Desilver. Published 6.8.2016. (Accessed 7/13/2016). <http://www.pewresearch.org/fact-tank/2016/06/08/increase-in-living-with-parents-driven-by-those-ages-25-34-non-college-grads/>

(121) Website: *The U.S. Department of Education at studentaid.ed.gov*. **The U.S. Department of Education offers low-interest loans to eligible students to help cover the cost of college or career school**. No author or publication date available. (Accessed 7/13/2016). <https://studentaid.ed.gov/sa/types/loans/subsidized-unsubsidized#how-much%29>

(122) Website: *The New York Times at nytimes.com*. **Why Science Majors Change Their Minds (It's Just So Darn Hard)**. Author Christopher Drew. 11/4/2011. (Accessed 7/13/2016). <http://www.nytimes.com/2011/11/06/education/edlife/why-science-majors-change-their-mind-its-just-so-darn-hard.html?_r=2&pagewanted=all>

(123) Website: *urbandictionary.com*. **Weeder Class**. Author: Cochiloco. Published: April 07, 2014. (Accessed 7/13/2016). <http://www.urbandictionary.com/define.php?term=Weeder+Class>

(124) Website: *PTC at ptc.com*. **High Dropout Rates Prompt Engineering Schools to Change Approach**. Author: Jon Marcus. Published on August 6, 2012. (Accessed 7/13/2016). <http://blogs.ptc.com/2012/08/06/high-dropout-rates-prompt-engineering-schools-to-change-approach/>

(125) Website: **List of U.S. states by income**. (2016, July 4). *In Wikipedia, The Free Encyclopedia*. Retrieved 18:06, July 13, 2016, from https://en.wikipedia.org/w/index.php?title=List_of_U.S._states_by_income&oldid=728368529

(126) Website: IPL2 at ipl.org. States Ranked by Size & Population. No author or publication date. (Accessed 7/13/2016). <http://www.ipl.org/div/stateknow/popchart.html>

(127) Website: *Massachusetts - The Official Website of the Executive Office of Labor and Workforce Development (EOLWD) at http://www.mass.gov/lwd/unemployment-insur/*. **Massachusetts Division of Unemployment Assistance - Massachusetts Labor Force**

Data and National Unemployment Rate. No author or publication date. (Accessed 7/14/2016). <http://lmi2.detma.org/lmi/Current_Month_unemploymnet.asp>

(128) Website: *Business Insider at businessinsider.com*. **Here's every US state's January unemployment rate**. Author: Andy Kiersz. Published Mar. 17, 2016. (Accessed 7/13/2016). <http://www.businessinsider.com/state-unemployment-map-january-2016-2016-3>

(129) Website: *Rowan University at rowan.edu*. **Bachelor of Science: Mechanical Engineering - Mechanical Engineering Required Courses**. No author or publication date. (Accessed 7/13/2016). <https://academics.rowan.edu/engineering/_docs/advising/curriculum-me2017.pdf>

(130) Website: *Consumer Financial Protection Bureau at consumerfinance.gov*. **Closing Disclosure Explainer**. No author or publication date. (Accessed 7/14/2016). <http://www.consumerfinance.gov/owning-a-home/closing-disclosure/>

(131) Website: **Regional accreditation**. (2016, June 17). In *Wikipedia, The Free Encyclopedia*. Retrieved 23:01, July 14, 2016, from https://en.wikipedia.org/w/index.php?title=Regional_accreditation&oldid=725735773

(132) Website: *Learning Online Blog at learningonlineblog.com*. **Websites for Teaching Calculus**. Author: Susan Brown. No publication date. (Accessed 7/14/2016). http://www.learningonlineblog.com/2014/03/22/websites-teaching-calculus/

(133) Journal Article: *Consumer Reports at consumerreports.org*. Published by Consumers Union of America. **Degrees of Debt and Regret**. Published 6/28/2016. (Accessed 7/21/2016) http://www.consumerreports.org/student-loan-debt-crisis/degrees-of-debt-and-regret/

(134) **Lemon Law**. (2016, June 6). *In Wikipedia, The Free Encyclopedia*. Retrieved 17:04, July 22, 2016, from

https://en.wikipedia.org/w/index.php?title=Lemon_law&oldid=72393
8188

(135) Website: *urbandictionary.com*. **helicopter parent**. Author:
Bruce. Published: August 30, 2005. (Accessed 8/1/2016).
<http://www.urbandictionary.com/define.php?term=helicopter%20par
ent>

(136) Website: *MindToMindParent.com*. **25 is the new 18**. Author:
donna@mindtomindparent.com. Published Oct 10, 2013. (Accessed
8/1/2016) <http://www.mindtomindparent.com/notes-to-self-blog/25-
is-the-new-adolescence/>

(137) Website: *US News and World Report* at usnews.com. **Experts:
'Weed Out' Classes Are Killing STEM Achievement**. Author: Jason
Koebler. Published Apr 19, 2012. (Accessed 8/4/2016.)
<http://www.usnews.com/news/blogs/stem-
education/2012/04/19/experts-weed-out-classes-are-killing-stem-
achievement>

(138) Website: *Tulane University at tulane.edu*. **Tulane Merit
Scholarship Continuation Requirements**. No author cited. Page last
updated 3/13/2015. (Accessed 8/4/2016.)
<https://www2.tulane.edu/financialaid/grants/mbrenew.cfm>

(139) Website: *Wayne State University at wayne.edu*. **Freshman
merit award renewal criteria**. No author or publication date cited.
(Accessed 8/4/2016) <http://wayne.edu/scholarships/freshmen/award-
renewal/>

(140) Website: *Louisiana State University at LSU.edu*. **University
Scholarship Retention Requirements**. No cited author or publication
date. (Accessed 8/4/2016.)
<https://sites01.lsu.edu/wp/financialaid/university-scholarship-
retention-requirements/>

(141) Website: *Stockton State University at stockton.edu*. **Freshman
Awards**. No cited author or publication date. (Accessed 8/4/2016.)
<http://intraweb.stockton.edu/eyos/page.cfm?siteID=64&pageID=114

(142) Website: *University of Central Florida at ucf.edu. **Provost Scholarship Renwal Eligibility***. No cited author or publication date. (Accessed 8/4/2016).
<http://finaid.ucf.edu/scholarships/provost_renewal.html>

(143) Website: *Arizona State University at asu.edu. **Renewal Criteria***. No cited author or publication date. (Accessed 8/4/2016.) https://students.asu.edu/scholarships/renewal

(144) Website: *Texas A&M University at tamu.edu. **Scholarships and Financial Aid, Texas A&M University 2014-2015***. No cited author or publication dates. (Accessed 8/4/2015)
<http://scholarships.tamu.edu/Scholarships/files/f6/f68be6e1-7d52-4236-84ea-578af50ebfa4.pdf>

(145) Website: Auburn University at auburn.edu. **Office of University Scholarships – Freshman Scholarship Guidelines**. No cited author or publication date. (Accessed 8/4/2016.)
<http://cps.auburn.edu/cps/Scholarships/documents/FreshmanScholarshipGuidelines.pdf>

(146) Website: *University of Washington at Washington.edu. **Low Scholarship***. No cited author or publication date. (Accessed 8/4/2016.)
<https://www.washington.edu/students/ugrad/advising/aif/lowschol.html>

(147) Website: *National Center for Education Statistics at nces.ed.gov. **STEM Attrition: College Students' Paths Into and Out of STEM Fields: Statistical Analysis Report***. Authors: Xianglei Chen and Matthew Soldner. Published November, 2013. (Accessed 8/5/2016. Esp. p14)
<http://nces.ed.gov/pubs2014/2014001rev.pdf>

(148) Website: *Business Insider at businessinsider.com. **Here's The Insane Amount Of Time Student-Athletes Spend On Practice***. Author: Peter Jacobs. Published Jan. 27, 2015. (Accessed 8/5/2016.)
<http://www.businessinsider.com/college-student-athletes-spend-40-hours-a-week-practicing-2015-1>

(149) Website: *The Center for Disease Control at cdc.gov.* **Attention Deficit/Hyperactivity Disorder - ADHD Symptoms Checklist**. No author or publication date cited. (Accessed 8/5/2016.) <http://www.cdc.gov/ncbddd/adhd/documents/adhd-symptom-checklist.pdf> and also <http://www.cdc.gov/ncbddd/adhd/diagnosis.html>

(150) Website: *Cornell University Law School Online Legal Dictionary at law.cornell.edu.* **Implied Warranty: Fitness for Particular Purpose**. No author or other publication cited. (Accessed 11 Sep 2016.) <https://www.law.cornell.edu/ucc/2/2-315>

(151) **Uniform Commercial Code**. (2016, August 30). In *Wikipedia, The Free Encyclopedia*. Retrieved 00:42, September 12, 2016, from https://en.wikipedia.org/w/index.php?title=Uniform_Commercial_Code&oldid=736809010

(152) Website: **Salary.com**. *Salary for Marketing Specialist*. No author cited. (Accessed 12 September 2016).

(153) Website: **Ted.Com**. **Presentation: How to expose the corrupt.** Filmed November 2009 at TEDxBerlin. Author: Peter Eigen. Filmed November 2009 at TEDxBerlin. (Accessed 9/13/2016.) <http://www.ted.com/talks/peter_eigen_how_to_expose_the_corrupt#>

(154) Website: **Ted.Com**. Presentation: **Sanjay Pradhan: How open data is changing international aid**. Filmed June 2012 at TEDGlobal 2012. Author: Sanjay Pradhan. (Accessed 9/13/2016.) < http://www.ted.com/talks/sanjay_pradhan_how_open_data_is_changing_international_aid/transcript?language=en>

(155) **Dennis Gabor**. Image Website: https://en.wikipedia.org/wiki/Dennis_Gabor#/media/File:Dennis_Gabor.jpg. (Accessed 10/3/2016.)

(156) Dennis Gabor Quotation. Website: http://quoteinvestigator.com/2012/09/27/invent-the-future/

(157) Website: *Pew Research*. **Increase in living with parents driven by those ages 25-34, non-college grads**. Author: Drew DeSilver. Source: <http://www.pewresearch.org/fact-tank/2016/06/08/increase-

in-living-with-parents-driven-by-those-ages-25-34-non-college-grads/> Published 6/8/2016. (Accessed 7/4/2017.)

(158) Website: http://www.nytimes.com/1998/03/27/nyregion/bernard-meltzer-dispenser-of-advice-on-radio-dies-at-81.html. *Bernard Meltzer, Dispenser Of Advice on Radio, Dies at 81.* **By Roberg MCG. Thomas Jr**. March 27, 1998. (Accessed 11/13/2016)

(159) Website: minneapolisfed.org Source: https://www.minneapolisfed.org/publications/the-region/till-college-do-us-part. *Phil Davies, Till College Do Us Part.* Published 2/11/2014. June 2014 Issue. (Accessed 11/21/2016)

(160) Website: *Socialmatter.net.* Source: http://www.socialmatter.net/2014/12/23/reproduction-and-its-substitute/. *"Reproduction and Its Substitute"* by Henry Dampier. Published December 23, 2014. Accessed 11/24/2016.

(161) Website: https://www.charteroak.edu/news/2016-itt-tech-transfer.cfm. No cited author or date. Accessed 2/20/2017. Let us help you transfer.

Omitted: (24) through (32), (49), (51) through (60), (67), (70), (74), (79), (81), (83), (85), (86), (89), (94), (97), (98), (108), (110), (117) (162)

Images Licensed from iStockPhotos.com.

Page	My Image Description (May differ from iStockPhoto description)	IStockPhoto ID
cover	Passed Out Studying	509292605
3	Challenges Ahead	155097607
6	Motorcycle Parts	496234162
8	Female Mechanic - Red Motorcycle	108274563
16	Business Woman in Office	530437128
16	Teen Girl Serves Fast Food	178381388
21	Chalkboard Friends Walk	584478142
25	Group Lecture	628483496
27	Approved 3d Gold Badge	492672844
28	Quality Ribbon Stamp	489518432
30	Woman Grinding in Workshop	509029818
32&34	Lecture Hall	140449928
34	Small Classroom	475762676
35	Communication Issue	679415368
36	Cancelled	636777624
39	College Campus Illustration	638392450
41	Texas Football Stadium	168324231
65	Tutoring In A Library	485422784
88	Professor Talking in Symbols	483506832
89	Approved Grunge Retro Ribbon Stamp	485099270
121	Brain Parts	498833195
125	Catching Up On Her Beauty Sleep	621836412
129	Builder Discussing Work With Apprentice	483717764
138	Cal Tech	458404527
138	Harvard	614119428
138	MIT's Ray and Maria Stata Center	592028852
152	Credit Transfer	668776944
171	Victorian Stationer's Shop	653942650
265	People Talking – Discussion	522726220
265	Mailing List	615252796

Appreciations

In creating this book, I am grateful for...

- Microsoft Word®, Evernote®, Paint.Net, MS Paint®, Visio®, Excel®, MS Project®, Google Calc®, FileZilla®.
- The publications who granted me permission to use their materials.
- "Ginger" grammar checker from GingerSoftware.com.
- Google Calc and Excel®.
- Dunkin' Donuts® Coffee
- iStockPhotos.com
- My Ikea® "Bekant" standing/sitting desk.
- Asus & Apple Computers; Acer, Qnix, and LG Monitors.
- Pandora® Radio for background music while writing.
- The Logitech Marble Mouse (Wish it had a blue tooth version.)

Index? What Index?

There is no index. If one was created post-publication, you will find it at www.thestemstudentsurvivalguide.com/index.

Proof

Made in the USA
Columbia, SC
04 August 2017